BASIC BIBLE SERIES

SERMON
ON THE MOUNT

WISDOM
OF THE
KINGDOM

BASIC BIBLE SERIES

SERMON
ON THE MOUNT

WISDOM
OF THE
KINGDOM

DAVID C. COOK PUBLISHING CO.
ELGIN, IL 60120

*This Basic Bible Series study was developed through the combined
efforts and resources of a number of David C. Cook's dedicated lesson
writers. It was compiled and edited by Jack Stewart, designed by
Melanie Lawson and Dawn Lauck, with cover art by Richard Sparks.*
  —Gary Wilde, Series Editor

Sermon on the Mount: Wisdom of the Kingdom

© 1986 David C. Cook Publishing Co., 850 North Grove Ave., Elgin, IL 60120. Printed in U.S.A.

Scripture quotations, unless otherwise noted, are taken from the Holy Bible: New International
Version, © 1973, 1978, 1984 by the International Bible Society, used by permission of
Zondervan Bible Publishers.

ISBN: 0-89191-521-4
Library of Congress Catalog Number: 86-70885

Matthew 7:24

Everyone who hears these words of mine and puts them into practice is like a wise man.

Contents

Introducing Matthew and the Sermon on the Mount

Matthew deserves its place as the first gospel and the first book of the New Testament. Matthew has been called the most widely read and most frequently quoted of the four evangelists. Because his gospel stresses the Kingship of Jesus Christ and our Lord's right to the throne of David, it has also been called the Royal Gospel.

Matthew's is the most Jewish gospel. It is his special concern to show how beautifully the ministry of Jesus Christ parallels and perfects the history of Israel. Matthew alone records the descent of the infant Jesus into Egypt (just as Israel went into Egypt). Matthew stresses the baptism of Jesus in the Jordan (as Israel was "baptized" in the Red Sea), the temptation of Jesus in the wilderness for 40 days (as Israel wandered and was tempted in the wilderness for 40 years), and so on. It is significant that Matthew tells us the words Jesus used to withstand Satan's temptations, for they are the same words Moses used when he preached to the Israelites. As you read the Gospel of Matthew you are made more and more aware that Jesus Christ was inaugurating a new Israel.

The first four chapters of Matthew clearly identify Jesus as the Servant Messiah of Isaiah, as King of the Kingdom, as the Messiah of whom the prophets speak, the Messiah of the God of Abraham and David, whose life manifests the same pattern as God's action in ancient Israel. His very life is an act of God; His life and actions fulfill the Law and Prophets just as, in the Sermon on the Mount, His teachings also will fulfill them.

Only with the introduction found in Matthew 1—4 do Jesus' claims and teachings in the Sermon on the Mount make sense. Without this special identity, the sermon is sheer arrogance. It does not stand alone as a piece of theology, ethics, or wisdom that could have come from just anyone's mouth. Its validity, authority, and particular meaning (as against its general tone) are dependent on the careful identification and authentication of Jesus as the Christ. This is outlined in the book of the "genealogy of Jesus Christ the son of David, the son of Abraham" (Mt. 1:1). By showing us the continuity of Jesus' life with the Old Testament, Matthew prepares us for Jesus' claims that His teachings are harmonious with it.

Matthew probably regarded the Sermon on the Mount, and especially the Beatitudes, as something of a parallel with Moses' ministry from Mt. Sinai. Christ is figured here as a supreme lawgiver, like Moses, yet much greater than Moses. He is also cast in the role of Wisdom, calling people to the discipline and obedience that leads to life and rest and peace (see Prov. 8:32-35, and Mt. 11:28-30).

Matthew also stresses the image of the master householder (see Mt. 20:1, KJV). In the Sermon on the Mount, then, we see Jesus as a master householder explaining to His servants the duties and privileges of living in His household, His Kingdom. The Sermon on the Mount is the "house rules" of the household. As the master householder treats all, so must each treat the others.

The Gospel of Matthew includes in 500 verses almost everything we find in Mark, though the stories are condensed. In addition, Matthew has a good deal of material similar to Luke (250 verses), while about 300 verses are unique to Matthew.

The book is built out of five discourses of Jesus alternating with blocks of narrative material. The five discourses are the Sermon on the Mount (chaps. 5—7), which is ethical; the sending of the Twelve (9:35-10:42), which is evangelistic; the parables of the Kingdom (chap. 13); relationships in the Kingdom (chap. 18), which is a rather ecclesiastical passage; and the second coming of Christ (chaps. 24, 25), which is eschatological and prophetic.

This systematic structure of the gospel may have contributed to its extensive use in the liturgy of the

Church over the ages. Incidentally, of the Gospels, only Matthew uses the word "church" (Mt. 16:18; 18:17). Matthew also draws special attention to the fulfillment of Old Testament prophecies by Jesus, the failure of first-century Jewish leadership, and the return of Christ. The Great Commission is found in Matthew 28. Probably this gospel was written in or near Palestine in the latter part of the first century for Jewish Christians in close contact with unbelieving Jews.

"When all else fails, read the directions." We may laugh at this caustic quote, but it applies to Christianity as much as to the use of a car or paintbrush. In the sayings of Jesus, and the Scriptures generally, we have the principles by which God wants us to live. To live in ignorance of them is to invite trouble.

Christ was zealous to instruct His followers in the way to live. In contrast to a religion that is all vague belief and no action, or all dutiful action and no underlying confidence in God Himself, Jesus teaches us that He is worthy of our confidence and will release His power in us. Nothing can be wiser than to learn His will and do it.

Before focusing on Matthew 5—7, try to read the entire gospel at least once. Matthew's Gospel is its own best commentary. The Sermon on the Mount is a table of contents for the entire gospel; and the gospel is an expanded commentary on every aspect of the Sermon on the Mount. The Beatitudes are the kernel, the "genetic code" for both the rest of the Sermon on the Mount and for the whole of Matthew. So if you are confused about the meaning of something in the Beatitudes, look to the rest of the Sermon on the Mount; if unclear about something in the Sermon on the Mount, look elsewhere in Matthew for an expansion or commentary—by parable or action.

Annie Dillard has said that if we really understood the God we claim to worship, we'd wear crash helmets to church—anticipating the release of His power. Approach the study of the Sermon on the Mount with the same excited caution: for here, if anywhere, is surely the life-changing power of the Word of God. Do not let your familiarity with this text blind you to it; do not assume ahead of time that you already know what it means.

Put on your crash helmet!

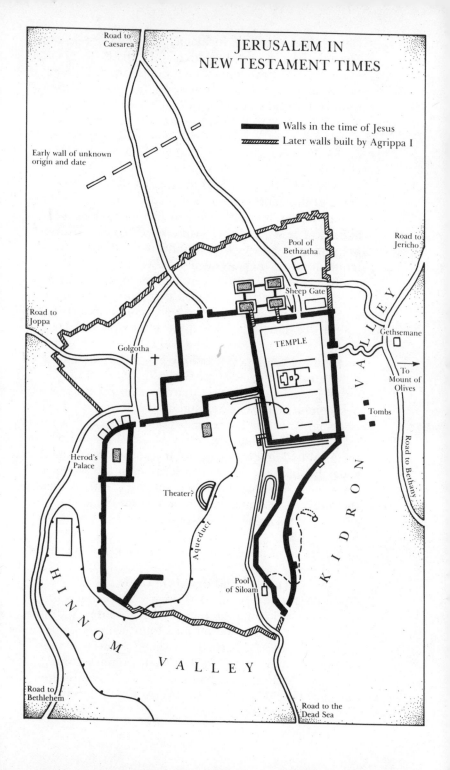

JERUSALEM IN
NEW TESTAMENT TIMES

Road to
Caesarea

━━━ Walls in the time of Jesus
▨▨▨ Later walls built by Agrippa I

Early wall of unknown
origin and date

Road to
Jericho

Pool of
Bethzatha

Sheep Gate

Road to
Joppa

TEMPLE

Golgotha

Gethsemane

To
Mount of
Olives

Tombs

Herod's
Palace

Theater?

K
I
D
R
O
N

V
A
L
L
E
Y

Road to
Bethany

Aqueduct

Pool
of Siloam

H
I
N
N
O
M

V A L L E Y

Road to
Bethlehem

Road to the
Dead Sea

1

The Beatific Life

Truth to Apply: Through His teaching in the Beatitudes, Christ calls me to a distinctively Christian life-style—one that gives a clear testimony to my world.

Key Verse: His disciples came to him, and he began to teach them (Mt. 5:1b, 2).

Malcolm Muggeridge, well-known English journalist and former agnostic, who in his later years converted to Christianity, compares the state of modern-day Christians to that of frogs in a pan of lukewarm water. If put in hot water, frogs will jump out of it. But if put in lukewarm water that is then very gradually heated, the frogs will grow accustomed to the higher temperatures, right up to the boiling point, when, of course, they die. Muggeridge suggests life in the Western world today is heating up, yet Christians are unaware of how serious the situation is. The changes are coming gradually and are often defended in the name of progress or greater tolerance. Foolishly, we live complacently in an increasingly evil environment.

Forty years ago the poet and scholar T. S. Eliot observed, "The problem of leading a Christian life in a non-Christian society is now very present to us." A college staff worker recently wrote in a personal letter, "I realize now more than ever that we are living in a post-Christian era, that we are facing a very paganized society."

There is no doubt that the time has arrived for Christians to live new and different lives and thereby challenge the world around them. But how can one be different without appearing too "weird" to gain the respect, and the listening ears, of friends and neighbors?

These familiar verses are known as the Beatitudes, after the Latin *beatus,* meaning, "happy, prosperous, blessed, fortunate." They describe the followers of Jesus Christ: how they must live, and how they shall be rewarded.

Note how beautifully the Beatitudes match each ascription ("Blessed are . . .") and promise ("for they shall receive . . . ."). The poor shall have a kingdom, the mournful shall be comforted, the meek shall own the whole earth, the hungry and thirsty shall be satisfied, the merciful shall be shown mercy, the pure shall see God, the peacemakers shall have many brethren, and the persecuted shall have, like the poor, a kingdom. The basic texts for the Beatitudes are Isaiah 61:1-4; 11:3b-5. Take a moment to read these passages. Notice the similarity of theme with the Beatitudes.

The Beatitudes begin and end with the promise of the Kingdom of Heaven (5:3 and 5:10). The fourth and the eighth Beatitudes have to do with righteousness (5:6 and 5:10).

We may observe, at least tentatively, that the first four Beatitudes describe the persecuted state of those who, helpless and vulnerable, wait for the salvation of God's Kingdom; the second four refer to the ethical qualities of the poor who are watching for God's Kingdom. Together, these characteristics are not new. Jesus did not invent them, as may be seen from their presence in Isaiah 11:3b-5; 61:1-4, and elsewhere in the Old Testament.

Matthew 5:3-6 corresponds closely to Luke's Beatitudes (Lk. 6:20-22). But whereas in Luke, Jesus then gives four woes (6:24-26), in Matthew, Jesus provides four additional Beatitudes. The first four are generally passive; the second four are generally more active.

Light on the Text

5:3   The "poor in spirit" are the same poor whom Luke describes in his parallel passage, Luke 6:20. In Jesus' day the word "poor" was loaded with religious meaning. It referred to the people who were not spiritually self-reliant and self-satisfied. The poor here are the resourceless and vulnerable afflicted of whom the prophets so often speak. American scholars W. F. Albright and C. S. Mann tell us, "The poverty described is that of the man fully conscious of the poverty of all human resource, and knowing his need and desire for God" (The Anchor Bible: *Matthew*). Perhaps the best illustration of Jesus' meaning is His own Parable of the Publican and the Pharisee (Lk. 18:10-13). These poor, like the publican, Jesus says, shall receive the Kingdom of Heaven. No special significance should be attached to the word "Heaven"; Matthew's Kingdom of Heaven is undoubtedly the same as Luke's Kingdom of God.

5:4   But what are we to mourn for, and thus be blessed? If we are right to think that Jesus had Isaiah 61 in mind, then it must be to mourn our present condition, to mourn the lack of righteousness in ourselves, our churches, our society, and to long for God to act. These shall be comforted by the one on whom the Spirit of the Lord has come.

5:5   Meekness comes next. For "meek" we might translate "humble," as over against the proud and hardhearted wicked (see Ps. 37:11; Zeph. 3:12). The meek are the ones who will remain and inherit the Promised Land— the Kingdom—after God's judgment has swept through.

5:6   Being poor, and therefore mournful, and therefore meek, implies the next Beatitude, "Blessed are those who hunger and thirst for righteousness, for they will be filled." Matthew 5:3, 4 stresses the theme of persecution, as also does 5:10-12. "Therefore it is likely that 'righteousness' here refers to right conduct on God's side, i.e., to the exercise of divine justice that finally results in the vindication longed for by the persecuted" (R. H. Gundry, *Matthew*). (Note that ordinarily "righteousness" in Matthew's Gospel refers to right conduct on the human side.)

   Thus to "hunger and thirst for righteousness" is here the longing of the poor, the mournful, and the meek for the salvation which they know can come only with the Kingdom of God. Perhaps the best expressions of this hunger are found in Mary's song (Lk. 1:46-55) and Zechariah's song (Luke 1:68-79).

5:7 Those who have remained meek and mournful despite affliction, and have continued to long for the righteousness of God, will have certain active characteristics as well. Remembering their own poverty of spirit and how they lamented over it, they will be forgiving to anyone asking for pardon. The tenderness of the Lord will be reflected in all their doings. As we learn in the Parable of the Unforgiving Servant (Mt. 18:23-35), this is one of the graces God most wants formed in us. (See also Matthew 6:14, 15; 12:7; 9:13, 27.)

5:8 Those who receive the righteousness of God shall also be pure in heart. This purity is the intensely moral and spiritual purity that seeks God. One thinks of our Lord's statement, "Love the Lord your God with all your heart, soul, and mind," and also when He said, "Seek first his kingdom and his righteousness" (Mt. 6:33). How fitting is the reward of the pure: "They will see his face" (Rev. 22:4).

5:9 "The peacemakers are not those who merely practice the negative virtue of non-resistance to evil. They are the people who overcome evil with good, and establish peace where there is discord and strife, who make up quarrels and reconcile enemies" (T. W. Manson, *The Sayings of Jesus*). Notice again how fitting their reward shall be: "They will be called the sons of God" (compare Mt. 5:45). Dr. Martyn Lloyd-Jones has written, "God gives us grace to see this blessed, glorious truth, and make us reflections, reproducers of the Prince of Peace, and truly children of the God of Peace" (*Studies in the Sermon on the Mount*).

5:10 We come full circle with the final Beatitude, the reward for which is the same as for the first—the Kingdom of Heaven. Judging from the commentary which follows this verse (in vss. 11-16), we are here dealing with a righteousness defined in terms of right conduct. Blessed are those who are persecuted because of their faithful obedience to God's ways. Notice the present tense: theirs *is* the Kingdom. This is the Kingdom which is "at hand"—which, with the coming of the Messiah, is now present. The Beatitudes are the vocabulary of the Kingdom. Where the Kingdom and righteousness of God are not the first priority, they are not understood or are scorned as impractical. But they are vital and everywhere present where the Kingdom is sought and its righteousness longed for. We shall gain more insight into their meaning as this study proceeds.

In summary, the blessed are those who practice righteousness, despite persecution, while waiting for and longing for the righteousness—that is, the salvation—of God.

We have difficulty finding a way to measure ourselves by the Beatitudes. These sayings are beautiful and profound—but what do they mean on Monday morning? To overcome this problem, try "translating" each of the Beatitudes into specific, relevant applications. (Of course, one could go on doing this forever and still not exhaust their meaning.) Here are some examples:

"Blessed are the poor in spirit": Happy are those who do not care to hang certificates of achievement on their walls.

"Blessed are those who mourn": The good are those who always end their day with regret for sins committed, and with a prayer of repentance.

"Blessed are the meek": Fortunate are those who ask good questions, listen carefully, and speak thoughtfully.

"Blessed are those who hunger and thirst for righteousness": Blessed are those who begin their days with prayers for pardon and for protection from the temptation to sin.

"Blessed are the merciful": Good are those who visit the people in jail, who show concern for the needy, the lonely, the distressed.

"Blessed are the pure in heart": Fortunate are those who live simple, uncluttered lives, and are free to give undivided attention to the things of God.

"Blessed are the peacemakers": Happy are those who support reconciliation, encourage communication, and pray for world leaders.

These examples only scratch the surface of possible applications. What are your ideas?

For Discussion

1. What similarities do you see among the first four characteristics of those who are "blessed"?

2. What would it mean in your life to be persecuted for righteousness' sake? To be poor in spirit? To hunger and thirst for righteousness? To be a peacemaker? To be merciful?

3. Often we gain insight into a thing by studying its opposite or its contrast. The world lives by a different set of Beatitudes from those of the Kingdom. Let your imagination and your sense of humor and irony suggest to you what would be the Beatitudes of the world. If you are in a group, compose a set of eight Beatitudes reflecting the values we often actually live by.

4. Suppose a soldier in wartime, or a penitentiary guard, or a tough labor-management negotiator heard these Beatitudes for the first time. How do you suppose such a person might respond? What would you reply?

Window on the Word

Persecution and Poverty of Spirit

On October 5, 1841, Father Dominic, almost 50 years old, was sent to England by his order in the late fulfillment of a vow he had made so long ago. . . . One day while he was walking through the village where the Passionists had secured a retreat house, a gang of toughs waylaid him. They began to throw stones, one of which struck him in the forehead, opening a gash. He stooped, retrieved the stone—the crowd hesitated—he winked, kissed the stone, and put it into his pocket, walking on.

2

Salt and Light

Truth to Apply: Living by the principles of the Beatitudes, I can become salt and light to the world around me.

Key Verse: Let your light shine before men, that they may see your good deeds and praise your Father in heaven (Mt. 5:16).

Mr. Roberts's house was in flames. The volunteer fire department sped to the scene and the fire fighters soon had a stream of water playing on the blaze. As they worked, Mr. Roberts's neighbors appeared and began shouting loud criticism of the fire fighters' methods. Their comments became so biting that the fire fighters turned the hose on them. The spectators, in response, charged the fire fighters. It took the local police department to quell the riot. Meanwhile, Mr. Roberts's house burned flat.

This incident actually took place in a New England town. The people in the community were pretty red faced—fire fighters, spectators, and all. Mr. Roberts wasn't too happy either.

There are many troublemakers in the world—people who enjoy starting something and then wading happily into the battle they have brought about. How can we be "salt and light" in such a world? What are your personal successes and failures in this endeavor?

Salt was greatly valued in the time of Christ. In the hot climate of Palestine, it was indispensable for the preservation of food in addition to its seasoning properties. It was also used occasionally as a medicine.

As well as salt, Christians are to be the light of the world. The symbolism, using light for good, and darkness for evil, is common in the Old Testament—indeed throughout the Jewish-Hellenistic world of that time.

Cities in Palestine were often set on a *tel*, or mound, that stood up above the surrounding land. The *tel* was often the site of a natural hill that had been built up by the ruins of successive cities, one level on top of another. Rising as it did above its surroundings, it was impossible to hide. The houses of the city were often built of white limestone, making the city even more conspicuous. The thought plainly is that Christians should be visible in order to fulfill their calling.

The first response of nearly everyone to the Beatitudes is: "Whoa! Wait a minute! This is not gonna work! Not in the world I live in!" And that was probably the common response in Jesus' day as well.
So His next words, now addressed directly to His listeners—"you," rather than the didactic "they"—deal precisely with this anticipated problem.

Light on the Text

5:10   Perhaps the best indicator that the Beatitudes are not about niceness or basic decency is this blessing on the persecuted. Christ here implies that the believer described in the Beatitudes will incur hatred and hostility. Jesus was not nailed to the cross because He was merely nice, or decent. It is something else, something higher, that makes a person persecuted. Our text describes it as "righteousness" (vs. 10). We have met this word in verse 6, "Blessed are those who hunger and thirst for righteousness"; and we meet it again in verse

20, ". . . unless your righteousness surpasses that of the Pharisees and the teachers of the law, you will certainly not enter the kingdom of heaven." It is clear in each instance the word means "exceptional purity" or "unique holiness." This righteousness, in other words, is specifically Christian. Thus Dr. Martyn Lloyd-Jones observes, "The righteous are persecuted because they are different. That was why the Pharisees and the scribes hated our Lord. It was not because he was good; it was because he was different" (*Studies*). The Christian will impress the world as uncommon, strange, peculiar, and therefore unwelcome. His or her righteousness will be, to the world, excessive, rigorous, certainly notable.

5:11   Christ mentions three ways the blessed ones will be persecuted. First, people may often revile them. This is reproach, name-calling, ridicule, mockery. Perhaps the clearest example of this sort of thing is found in Matthew 27, where we read how the soldiers placed on Jesus a scarlet robe, a crown of thorns, a reed in His hand, and mocked Him, saying, "Hail, King of the Jews!" (Mt. 27:29). We read also that the crowds "hurled insults at him, shaking their heads and saying . . . 'He saved others . . . but he can't save himself' " (Mt. 27:39, 42). Even the thieves did the same.

Second, people may assault the Christians—actually harm their bodies and possessions. Read Paul's list of his sufferings (II Cor. 11:23-27). Tertullian, a Church Father of about A.D. 200, is credited with saying, "The blood of martyrs is the seed [of the Church]."

Third, Christians will find themselves slandered. Lies will be told about them. The early Christians were said to be atheists because they refused to worship idols; cannibals, because they partook of the body and blood of Christ; immoral, because they celebrated love feasts in secret places; and unpatriotic, because they refused to offer incense to the emperor. Christians were blamed for the burning of Rome during the reign of Nero. Paul frequently had to refute spurious charges against his character (II Cor. 11:17, 18; Gal. 1:10).

5:12   Christians will "rejoice and be glad" when they have these hardships. These experiences will be a proof, or confirmation, that they are part of the household of God—for the servant is not better than the master. The saints of God have always suffered for God. "In fact, everyone who wants to live a godly life in Christ Jesus will be persecuted" (II Tim. 3:12). But the loss hardly compares with the reward.

5:13   Christ now compares His followers to salt. Some have responded that Jesus is using a figure of speech that has no parallel in nature, as if to say, "Salt does not lose its saltiness, but supposing it did, with what would it be salted?" But this answer is unconvincing, for Jesus appears to be referring to actual and familiar experience.

Everyone agrees that salt, as pure salt, does not lose its saltiness. What must be meant is the contamination of salt by foreign substances. The shores of the Dead Sea, conveniently located for Judeans, yielded usable salt. But it also produced just such an impure and worthless variety as Jesus here mentions. Surely that is the salt Jesus means. It was of the rock or fossil variety, and was often so mixed with other chemicals that there was nothing one could do with it except kill unwanted vegetation on roads and walkways (see Ezek. 47:11).

When pure, however, salt was an invaluable commodity and served as a symbol of all that is good and wholesome. Prof. R. K. Harrison (*The New Bible Dictionary*) informs us that salt was not only a seasoning and a preservative; it was also used as a symbol of fidelity when contracts were ratified.

5:14   The metaphor of light accents the outer and more visible elements of Christianity. Salt is an image of the inner aspect; but light suggests a visible work and a spoken word. Believers must show the Gospel of Christ to the world. Jesus says they are to be like a city and a lamp.

"A city on a hill cannot be hidden." The backbone of Palestine is a mountainous chain of hills and rugged terrain extending intermittently from Galilee in the north to Judea in the south. The peaks in Upper Galilee, rising to over 3,000 feet, present one with a view of even the Mediterranean Sea. Of Jerusalem, built on a mountain surrounded by mountains, the psalmist sings, "It is beautiful in its loftiness, the joy of the whole earth" (48:2). Set on one of these hills, any city, and certainly Jerusalem itself, would be radiant.

"Neither do people light a lamp and put it under a bowl." The simple Jewish peasant lit this lamp for illumination, placing it on a shelf on the central beam of the one-room house, where it gave light "unto all."

It follows that Christian deeds are to be visible. This does not mean they are to be showy or spectacular, but evident to anyone who wishes to see. It also follows that the Christian message is to be *heard*. People are to give the glory to God the Father. This is done as the Gospel is clearly expressed through, and alongside, the works.

Evangelism in the Greek New Testament

When Christians are salt and light in the world, they are directly involved in evangelism. The word "evangelism" can't be found in the King James Version, although "evangelist" is used several times. However, the Greek New Testament uses this term, or one related to it, over 100 times.

Euangelion is cited on over 70 occasions, and in each case it has been translated "Gospel." Lexicographers note that originally this meant a reward for good news, then came to designate the good news itself. W. E. Vine states: "In the New Testament it denotes the good tidings of the Kingdom of God and of salvation through Christ, to be received by faith, on the basis of His expiatory death, His burial, resurrection, and ascension" (*An Expository Dictionary of New Testament Words*).

Paul the apostle defined the "Gospel" as having to do with Christ's death, burial, and resurrection (I Cor. 15:1-4). It is the wonderful news about God's Son.

Paul's helper, Timothy, was instructed by the apostle to "do the work of an evangelist" (II Tim. 4:5). The *euangelistes* is simply the bearer of good news. Joseph Henry Thayer noted: "This name is given in the New Testament to those heralds of salvation through Christ who are not apostles" (Acts 21:8; Eph. 4:11).

Euangelizo is found over 50 times and has been rendered "declare," "preach," "bring good tidings," "declare glad tidings," "preach the Gospel." In Arndt and Gingrich's lexicon it is rendered: "bring or announce good news." The note is added: "mostly specifically of the divine message of salvation, the Messianic proclamation."

From strict exegesis of the New Testament, evangelism has to do with the preaching of salvation in Jesus Christ.

For Discussion

1. How is it that by being merciful, pure in heart, or a peacemaker, one can be the salt of the earth, that is, add savor to life, or preserve life from rot and spoilage? What might this mean in your office, on the job, in your family life, or at church?

2. How are we to reconcile verses 5:11, 12 with 5:16? Are we to expect persecution for righteousness's sake; or that people will, seeing our good works, give glory to our Heavenly Father? Or both?

3. What is the difference between your "light" and your "good works"? What is this light by which others are able to see your good works?

Window on the Word

The Alexandrian Ministry

During a plague in Alexandria, Egypt, in the latter part of the third century, "the Christians distinguished themselves by selfless behavior, tending the sick and burying the dead while the pagan inhabitants fled like panic-stricken animals. There were plenty of cases where sick pagans were abandoned by their own families in the streets, only to be picked up and nursed by Christians. Quite a number of Christians who could have escaped the plague by leaving the city stayed behind on purpose to look after the sick and dying, and eventually died of the disease themselves. Remember, too, that some of those sick and dying pagans who were cared for had probably been members of the Alexandrian mob which ten years before had been on the rampage, lynching any Christians that they could find" (M. A. Smith, *From Christ to Constantine*).

3

The Lord and the Law

Truth to Apply: Because Jesus fulfilled the Law on my behalf, I can joyfully make righteous living my daily goal.

Key Verse: Do not think that I have come to abolish the Law or the Prophets; I have not come to abolish them but to fulfill them (Mt. 5:17).

"Why bother to have children learn the Ten Commandments? We are Christians, not Jews!" This was the observation of a well-meaning but misguided father when he learned that his daughter had been learning the Ten Commandments in Sunday school.

Many people are less open about it, but they really feel we have somehow left behind God's Law, as expressed in the Old Testament. They mistakenly set the teachings of Jesus against the Law as if the latter were as obsolete as last year's tax forms.

But does not modern life bear tragic witness to what happens when people in large numbers set aside the Law of God? What specific evidence of this do you see in your own community?

These four verses are as crucial as any in the Sermon on the Mount. In them Jesus declares His relationship to the Law and the Prophets, and to the Kingdom. Furthermore, He announces what this means for His listeners and their approach to the Law.

All this, like the preceding Beatitudes, is in the form of announcement, of prologue. Nothing is completely spelled out or explained. We shall have to wait for the rest of the book to unfold in order to understand fully what Jesus says here. (From 5:17-20 alone, for example, it is not possible to say exactly how Jesus' righteousness of the Kingdom exceeds that of the Pharisees. This first becomes clear only in 5:21—7:11.

And what was He announcing? That He, not the Pharisees or human traditions, is the true interpreter of the Law. To the poor who were scorned by the Pharisees and scribes as hopelessly lax in obeying the letter of the Law, who lacked the education and the money to keep the fastidious and exhaustive details of Pharisaic obedience (see Mt. 23), to such as these, Jesus' words were both good news and bad news. The bad news is that, yes, your righteousness must exceed that of the Pharisees. Amazing! The good news is that unlike the complicated rules of the Pharisees' righteousness, Jesus' righteousness is close at hand, even to poor ordinary people. It consists of trust and obedience of Jesus' words.

Before He starts into His teachings on the Law, Jesus denies the charge that He is abolishing the Law. Jesus claimed that His teachings were "in absolute harmony with the entire teaching of the Old Testament Scriptures" (D. Martyn Lloyd-Jones, *Studies in the Sermon on the Mount*).

Light on the Text

5:17, 18 Jesus used the word "fulfill" to mean to give full obedience to everything stated in the Holy Scriptures. And Jesus did fulfill the Scriptures in every aspect. He perfectly obeyed all of its holy demands. He obeyed all its legal demands against sin by His sacrificial death. He filled with meaning all of the Old Testament prophecies and types concerning the Messiah. It could be said that Jesus kept the moral law, paid the price of judicial Law (as our substitute), and personified the ceremonial law.

Jesus spoke of the eternal nature of the Law when He said not one jot or tittle would pass away unfulfilled. The jot (or *yohd*) was the smallest letter of the Hebrew alphabet, looking like our modern-day apostrophe. The tittle was the smallest part of certain individual letters and would roughly correspond to the projecting foot of a letter. It was sort of like the difference between our capital O and Q. Jesus placed such high respect and authority upon the Scriptures that He said not even its smallest detail would pass away without being fulfilled.

Next, Jesus asserted that His teaching, being in complete harmony with the true meaning of the Old Testament Scriptures, was in contrast to the teachings of the scribes and Pharisees. These persons were the leading Jewish religious groups of the first century and they had made an indelible mark upon all Judaism. They viewed the Word of God, given in the Old Testament, primarily as law. They wanted the Law, often given in general principles, to be explicitly worked out in minute detail so that the religious person would know exactly what to do, or not to do, in every situation.

For example, when the Law said you should not work on the Sabbath, it became necessary to define "work" and "Sabbath." This was meticulously done by the lawyers or the scribes. Working meant carrying a package, writing, or healing. Religion became an ongoing, never-ending definition of what the Law permitted or prohibited. William Barclay writes: "So they spent endless hours arguing whether or not a man could or could not lift a lamp from one place to another on the Sabbath, whether a tailor committed a sin if he went out with a needle in his robe, whether a woman might wear a brooch or false hair, even if a man might go out on the Sabbath with artificial teeth or an artificial limb, if a man might lift his child on the Sabbath day" (*Matthew*).

For the scribes this was the essence of religion. Theirs was a religion of legalism, petty rules and regulations that often actually perverted the true intent of God's revealed will. The Pharisees were the "separated ones" who, in highly systematic fashion, attempted to keep all of the scribal law, which at that time was chiefly oral. It was only written down as the *Mishnah* in the third century A.D.

It was this type of religion that Jesus forcefully opposed. He was not rejecting the Law of God but the law of people. This law—the traditions of these religious leaders—actually perverted and often reversed the true intent of the Law. Jesus taught that no one was righteous before God without love for, and faith in, God (Lk. 18:9-14; Mt. 22:34-40). Merit (keeping the Law) is not the way to salvation, according to Jesus and all New Testament writers. Forgiveness of sins and the gift of eternal life are experienced through mercy, not merit.

"Not one jot or tittle" refers to even the smallest part of the Law and the Prophets. Every particle of these will be fulfilled. The end of time is meant by the words "until Heaven and earth disappear."

The righteousness of the "Pharisees and teachers of the law" was a misplaced emphasis on scrupulous fulfillment of the many traditional interpretations of the Law. They lost sight of the intended meaning of God's Law and concentrated instead on keeping human regulations that had actually become a substitute for it. The scrupulous tithing of herbs grown in their gardens became more important than justice, fairness, and mercy in relations with people (Mt. 23).

5:19   Here Jesus focuses on the moral law, which the leaders of the day had corrupted. For instance, we learn in Matthew 15 that they taught if a man ceremonially committed his estate to God, he was freed of the responsibility of honoring his parents by supporting them. Further, by their actions, the religious leaders reflected a hypocrisy exactly opposite to the sincerity of the Law of Moses. (See Christ's attacks on hypocrisy in Matthew 6.)

5:20   This verse would be a shock to many, because the Pharisees were believed to represent the peak of spirituality.

Now that Christ has died for us, the Law's rules for sacrifice and ceremonial ritual have been fulfilled (see Heb. 9). This means Christians need not repeatedly sacrifice animals on an altar to make atonement for their sins. Nor is it necessary that they observe the Passover feast, as people were required to do under the Old Covenant. Instead, people of the New Covenant observe the ordinance of Communion to commemorate Jesus' sin-canceling death on the cross. Thus the coming of Jesus Christ has completed these portions of the Law. What remains in force is God's moral law, summarized in the Ten Commandments, Exodus 20:1-17. This is what must be kept by those who would be great in the Kingdom of Heaven, where "Your will be done on earth as it is in heaven" (Mt. 6:10).

For Discussion

1. What has Jesus said or done to even suggest that He might have "come to abolish the Law or the Prophets"? Why does He feel the need to begin with such a denial? Is He merely anticipating His teachings in Mt. 5:21—7:11?

2. What hints do you find in the rest of Matthew's Gospel as to what Jesus meant by fulfilling the Law and the Prophets? What is Jesus doing here if not "breaking" or "relaxing" (RSV) one of the Commandments and teaching others to do the same? If Jesus is here fulfilling the Law, explain how.

3. What distinguishes "breaking" or "relaxing" a Commandment, (which is what Jesus goes on to refute in Mt. 5:21-48) from doing its true and full intent?

Window on the Word

Oh, how I love your law! I meditate on it all day long.

In a series of church member interviews, the following question was asked: "When do you study the Bible?"

A housewife: "After the kids get off to school, I eat my breakfast, drink my coffee, and then spend a half hour with the Bible. Right now I'm going through Isaiah at two chapters a day. I ask God to show me something significant, and when I see it I meditate on that."

A high school student: "I spend the fifteen minutes just before I go to bed each night. I'm reading through the New Testament in *The Living Bible,* a couple of chapters a night. I read, then ask myself, 'Now, what is this saying?' When I see its meaning, I try to apply it to my life, then I pray."

A businessman: "I spend my noon hours alone as a rule, so I've been reading the Bible each day. In the course of the week I always include the passage we're studying on the following Sunday."

A sixth grader: "I read the Bible each morning after breakfast before I go to school. My brothers leave before I do, so the house is quiet."

A retired businessman: "I lead our adult class at church. It is the only group in church that stresses study of the Bible, so I feel especially responsible. I usually spend each evening studying the passage for the coming Sunday, making notes, and deciding how to present the material. Frequently, my wife and I have the radio on to a baseball game, but this is in the background and it doesn't seem to interfere with my study."

4

Dangerous Anger

Truth to Apply: Christ calls me to deal constructively with my anger.

Key Verse: Anyone who is angry with his brother will be subject to judgment (Mt. 5:22).

"Violence," said Rap Brown, "is as American as apple pie." If this is true, then God's Word has much to say to the American way of life.

The history of the United States, for example, has been filled with violence and the taking of human life. The country came into existence through a rebellion. Settlers drove hundreds of thousands of native Americans from their lands or killed them outright. Estimates range from ten to twenty million for the number of Africans who were captured, tortured, killed, and enslaved because of the country's demand for a free labor supply. Violence also attended the rise of the labor movement, the black drive for civil rights, and global involvements due to territorial or economic expansion.

Violent crimes in both Canada and the U.S. have increased sharply in the past two decades. Cities are called "jungles" or "armed fortresses." Every day the newspapers tell of senseless killings that sicken every sensitive person. This is not even taking into account the rash of international acts of terrorism.

Television violence is given much publicity but little is done to lessen it. A study by the National Association for Better Broadcasting estimates the average child sees 13,000 violent deaths on television during the formative years of 5 to 15.

Every Christian can see the common disregard of the Sixth Commandment. We should also be able to see in ourselves the actual and potential anger that is the root cause of murder. How can we refrain from murdering people in our hearts?

By the middle ages, the Ten Commandments had been established as the basic text of Christian ethics. Each Commandment was given first a negative injunction ("thou shalt not . . ."), which was always followed by its corresponding positive implication ("therefore, thou shalt . . ."). In effect, this amounted to saying that not only are you not to take your neighbor's life, but you are bound to do whatever you can to enhance and perpetuate his or her life. This Christian ethical development is solidly based in Jesus' own teachings in Matthew 5:21-26, where He goes beyond the strict prohibition of murder to enjoin His followers to be reconciled, to become friends with an estranged and perhaps hated brother or sister. And Jesus, in this first of a series of "you-have-heard-but-I-say" statements in chapter 5, is well supported by the Law in going beyond the negative prohibition to a positive injunction: "Do not hate your brother in your heart . . . but love your neighbor as yourself" (Lev. 19:17, 18).

Moreover, our relationship to our "brother" is a measure or index of our relationship to our Father: "First go and be reconciled to your brother; then come and offer your gift" to your Father (see Mt. 6:14, 15; and 18:23-25).

Light on the Text

5:21   Here Jesus is quoting Old Testament authority: Exodus 20:12, 13 and Numbers 35:30, 31.

5:22   "'Raca,' an Aramaic word, means 'empty head,' and is often mentioned in rabbinic writings as a common term of abuse" (*A New Bible Commentary*, Zondervan). To assault or berate someone is a form of violence forbidden by this Commandment. "'Raca' expresses contempt for a man's head: you stupid!" (Bruce).

The expression "you fool" needs to be understood in the light of Jewish tradition. In their way of thinking, "fool" was a suitable synonym for practical atheism (see Ps. 14:1). Thus, religious slander also came within the purview of Jesus' understanding of the Commandment.

That Jesus Himself uses this same term— "fools!" (Mt. 23:17)—suggests that what Jesus intends here is to forbid hatred and the desire to abuse another person. In Matthew 23:17, Jesus uses the term as a prophet—calling the Pharisees to repentance.

The punishment for breaking this Commandment was far greater than the Jews were willing to admit. It was not merely the punishment of the Sanhedrin, the judicial council of the Jews, but the punishment of hell fire.

By the time of Jesus, the Commandment had been greatly perverted by the Jewish rabbinical tradition. This perversion took two forms. First, the Commandment was limited to actual murder. The Law of God was thus reduced from a principle governing all of life to a legal statute in Israel. Second, the punishment for murder was restricted to the temporal courts. The judgment Jesus speaks of is what one would face in a Jewish court of law.

5:23 When one becomes aware of breaking this Commandment, whether by insulting word or vicious deed, there is a responsibility to repent and to seek reconciliation with the other party. Such reconciliation will involve apologies, an attempt to make restitution wherever possible, and a deep-seated desire to overcome the enmity built up by the hurtful actions. Jesus insisted that this repentance and reconciliation takes priority over worship.

5:25, 26 Jesus went on to indicate the importance of reconciliation in human relationships. The kind of violence spoken of in the Sixth Commandment leads naturally to the perpetuation of violence, even to escalation of it. Trying to get even with your accuser, or with one who has hurt you, continues the enmity, most likely leading to more violence.

R. C. H. Lenski, in his *Interpretation of St. Matthew's Gospel* (Lutheran Book Concern), writes, "By saying that anger is equal to murder and worthy of the death penalty, and an angry epithet likewise, Jesus shows how

God judges these sins; and when for a similar epithet he decrees hell fire, he shows that hell is the penalty for all these sins in the judgment of God, beginning with anger and on through to murder."

If a relationship between two persons is damaged by anger, true spiritual worship acceptable to God is impossible (vss. 23, 24). We should take positive steps to eliminate anger, or any cause for it, by seeking reconciliation with a person we have wronged. That is, we must not only stay free from anger and abusive talk ourselves, but we must also do what we can to remove anger in others. It is more important to take the initiative in reconciliation "than to preserve the smoothness and dignity of the altar rites" (Floyd V. Filson, *A Commentary on Matthew*).

Some scholars think the last two verses in this section are misplaced (compare Lk. 12:58, 59, where they occur in another setting). But they do relate to the topic at hand. If they are taken in a literal sense, they stress the urgency of reconciliation, describing another way to remove a cause of anger in a person we have wronged and so save ourselves from added distress. If these verses are viewed as a parable, they teach that a believer should "be reconciled to his brother while there is still time, in order that his brother may not be his accuser at the Last Judgment" (*The Layman's Bible Commentary*).

Thou Shalt Not Kill

"Human life is emphatically declared to be sacred," wrote G. Campbell Morgan in *The Ten Commandments*. "It is a divine creation, mysterious and magnificent in its genesis and possibility, utterly beyond the control or comprehension of any human being. It is, therefore, never to be taken at the will of one who can by no means know the full meaning of its being. This command not to take life is, therefore, based on the truths that *God alone gives human life* and *God alone has the right to take human life*."

We must be clear that the word "kill" is better translated for us as "murder." The English language distinguishes between different kinds of death and so does the Hebrew. If "kill" were meant in the broadest sense, the Commandment would exclude slaughter of cattle for meat or swatting a fly for sanitation purposes. What it does prohibit is the violent, willful, and malicious assault on the life of another. It also guards against an individual's taking the law into his or her own hands. An injustice against someone should not be corrected by an individual acting with unilateral authority. Rather, only the community and the properly ordained judicial procedure should deal with offenses that might lead someone to kill another in vengeance.

We can, therefore, understand that in Israel all killing was not prohibited or considered out of the will of God. Specifically, God ordered certain offenses in the nation of Israel punished by death: murder, child sacrifice, adultery, homosexual acts, and idolatry, for example. Thus, since God gave both the Sixth Commandment and the death penalty for certain crimes, some have concluded that He did not intend the Commandment to eliminate capital punishment. Furthermore, the Lord on numerous occasions ordered the Israelites to do battle. Thus, war was apparently not excluded by the Sixth Commandment. What is your view on these issues?

For Discussion

1. We commonly hear it said, "He made me angry," or "She made me furious when she . . . ." This puts the burden upon the offender. But in the Sermon on the Mount, Jesus speaks repeatedly to the offended one: the persecuted, the one who is struck or coerced to do something. Do you agree that the offended party is the one who should take the first step toward reconciliation? How does this actually work in everyday life?

2. Why does reconciliation with a brother or sister take precedence over offering worship to God? How could we put this principle into practice in our churches? What happens when we ignore it?

3. Verses 5:25, 26 suggest that if opportunities for reconciliation are not quickly taken, then the situation can become irredeemable, that is, "you will never get out." What do you think? What has your experience taught you about what Jesus is saying?

Window on the Word

Anger Can Kill!

"An evangelist was in a certain city for a two-week meeting. He was asked by a friend to visit a woman in the hospital. She was dying with cancer. On the first visit, the patient was expecting the minister to pray for her. However, he felt the restraining of the Lord, 'Don't pray for her.' He was obedient and said to the woman, 'I'm sorry. I cannot pray for you.' She responded somewhat disdainfully. Upon being asked to return, the evangelist did so. Again the Lord warned him not to pray for the woman. This time he asked her, 'How are you related to your pastor?' "This question brought about a torrent of pent-up anger. 'Don't talk to me about him. I hate him! You don't know what he did to me. Don't ask me to forgive him!' It was later learned that for some fifteen years the woman had been harboring and nursing hate mixed with anger. She didn't want to give up her feelings, either.

"Further urging from family and friends resulted in still another visit to the hospital. This time the patient was hanging onto life by a bare thread. Reaching for the hand of the evangelist, she whispered, 'Call my pastor.' The pastor came; forgiveness was effected; there was joy and reunion. There was also healing as a result of that breaking and forgiveness. Do you catch the meaning of 'shutting up until the last farthing has been paid'?" (From *The King and You* by Bob Mumford, copyright 1974 by Fleming H. Revell Company. Published by Fleming H. Revell Company. Used by permission.)

5

Passions Under Control

Truth to Apply: I can learn to restrain my passions, rather than wrong my neighbor.

Key Verse: Do not commit adultery (Ex. 20:14; Mt. 5:27b).

We live in an age supersaturated with sex. We are constantly exposed to sexual stimuli. Sex forms the basis of a large percentage of our advertising: every type of product, from milk to deodorants to razor blades to automobiles, is sold by using sexual appeals. Sexual themes are frequently used in literary and dramatic productions, often presented in extremely explicit ways. At the far end of this spectrum lies a flood of hard-core pornography.

Sex is dealt with in an increasingly mechanical fashion. Many articles and books treat sex primarily as a technique to be learned. Such emphasis on technique can bring about a deemphasis on the love relationship, so that the true value of sex is lost.

We also have the idea of "the therapy of adultery," made popular by soap operas, novels, and even some psychiatrists. This is as dangerous as taking one kind of poison as an antidote for another.

The modern sex scene is not a pleasant one. It shows that we are far from the sexual paradise many expected when Victorianism was finally killed. We have many problems today that were not present in the past. Could these problems be dealt with from a Christian view of sex if such a view were more adequately and clearly presented? How would this actually work?

Some people consider the Bible's view of sexuality to be restrictive and secretive. This can only come from lack of familiarity with what the Bible actually has to say about sex. The Bible recognizes sex as more than a few organs in a human body or certain actions in human life. Sexuality is a part of the mystery of humanity. From Creation, the Bible gives men and women a sexual identity. They are intended by God to be complementary to one another. Sexuality is treated as a legitimate and necessary part of personhood.

The Bible's view of sex is neither repressive nor libertarian. The historical portions deal with sex matter-of-factly. In its poetic sections the Bible deals with sex in what tends to be romantic, and honest language. Descriptions of sex in the Song of Solomon contain imagery that is both beautiful and explicit.

The Bible constantly assumes that sex is related to personality. It is a form of relationship. Notice the Old Testament word used for sexual intercourse—"know" (see Gen 4:1, 17, 25). Through sex, a person comes to know his or her partner in a way that cannot be discovered otherwise. Consequently, the Biblical view of sex is that its use is to be governed by its effects on personality. The proper use of sex is covenantal. It is made within a relationship between two people who have committed themselves to one another. Improper sex is manipulative; in it one or both sexual partners use the other to satisfy their own needs.

Just as the Sixth Commandment (Thou shalt not murder) had been limited to the act of murder itself, so the Seventh Commandment (Thou shalt not commit adultery) had been restricted to the act itself. Jesus extended both Commandments to prohibit the hatred and the lust lying at the root of both.

Shortly before the time of Christ, the Old Testament grounds for divorce, indicated by the phrase "something indecent about her" (Deut. 24:1), had come to be interpreted in two different ways. "The school of Shammai interpreted it of unfaithfulness only, while the school of Hillel extended it to anything unpleasing to the husband" (*The New Bible Dictionary*, ed. Douglas). Jesus was apparently more of the Shammai school of thought. Further, He exhorted husbands to be merciful to their wives (and wives to their husbands) by forgiving rather than divorcing, even when they had grounds for divorce.

Thus, in verses 27-32 we find both judgment and mercy: judgment and discipline of our own members; mercy for offenders of this Commandment.

Light on the Text

5:27   So far, Jesus has simply repeated the Old Testament Commandment against adultery. David C. Hill (*The Gospel of Matthew*) says this refers not to preserving oneself from impurity, so much as to avoiding breaking into another person's marriage; not to the natural desire for a man or a woman, but to lustful desire for another's spouse.

5:28   It is not that Jesus isn't concerned with the outward act—He is. But knowing, as He later says, that all evil comes from the heart (Mt. 15:17-20), He seeks to drive the Law deeper, to write it, as Jeremiah says, upon their hearts, so that His followers may be pure both inside and out, in thought as well as deed.

5:29, 30   Origen, one of the early Church Fathers, took this passage so seriously that he castrated himself, cutting off the member which "caused him to sin."

Most commentators point out that Jesus refers to the *right* eye and the *right* hand—considered the most valuable. In this way, they feel, Jesus is symbolically saying, "Remove anything from its place of influence which causes you to sin, even if it is your most precious belonging."

Jesus only mentions one eye and one hand whereas every normal human has two of each. If the cause of sin were literally in these physical parts, both eyes and both hands would need to be removed, for the left eye and the left hand could prove as offensive as the right ones. The eye of lust and the hand of greed work from the heart, the inner self, and can appear as easily on the left as on the right.

Jesus would be inconsistent if He were giving a physical solution to what He defines as a heart problem. The reason Jesus uses the language about self-mutilation is to make His point forcefully, namely, that sin is a dreadful sickness demanding a drastic solution.

We must take a serious look at Jesus' admonition to maim a part of ourselves. The salvation of the whole person may require the sacrifice of part of that person. Passing through the narrow gate, shorn of those "members" which cause us to sin, we may, in a sense, enter God's Kingdom maimed.

Recognition of beauty, or the attraction to a person of the opposite sex, is not sin. Nor is sexual desire itself sinful. It is the lust to satisfy the sexual impulse outside of the marriage relationship that is wrong. When such desire comes, the temptation must be firmly resisted, and the thought brought captive to the mind of Christ (II Cor. 10:5).

Jesus teaches us that the Law of God is not to be interpreted in a narrow way as if each one dealt with only one specific sin. Rather, each Commandment is a principle governing a basic area of life. Understanding those principles and applying them to specific situations is an important ethical challenge for every Christian.

Jesus restated the Commandment in a way that emphasized its depth and breadth. First of all, it is obvious from the statement that He was speaking to men, in distinction to the emphasis on women already pointed to. Yet by speaking to all men He does not mean women are excluded. He spoke directly to men because they needed to hear it most in that society.

In the second place, Jesus' statement deals with the heart of a man—thoughts as well as actions. The man who sees a woman as a sex object rather than a person is already guilty of violating the Seventh Commandment.

5:31 Again, Jesus repeats the Old Testament command. Remember, the original aim of this command was a merciful one: to prevent men from merely taking women and discarding them when they wished. Its focus is the welfare of the woman.

5:32 Though the phrase "except for marital unfaithfulness" is implied in Deuteronomy 24:1, it does not appear in the parallel passages in Mark 10:10 and Luke 16:18. This may indicate that Matthew's special "concern lies . . . on husbandly compassion as a deterrent to divorce" (R. H. Gundry, *The Gospel of Matthew*). Blessed are the merciful.

By divorcing his wife, a man "causes" her to commit adultery, presumably, because she will remarry.

For Discussion

1. Since we are not meant to literally "gouge out" our right eye or cut off our right hand, what does Matthew 5:29, 30 mean? What would it mean to sacrifice something of great value to you in order to avoid being "thrown into hell"?

2. Why is it often hard for Christians to forgive themselves for sexual sin? Why is it often hard for Christians to forgive the sexual sins of others?

3. What Biblical counsel could you give someone tempted to commit adultery?

4. How might someone who embodies the Beatitudes (Mt. 5:3-10) respond differently from a legalistic or Pharisaic person when sinned against by adultery?

5. What should a church do if one of its members is guilty of adultery? If the guilty member repents?

Window on the Word

The Archbishop Burns His Hand

"In the year 1556, Thomas Cranmer, Archbishop of Canterbury, was burned at the stake. Before the fire was kindled he requested that his right hand be burned first. The reason for his strange request is that he was repenting of the recantations he had signed under pressure from Queen Mary, and he wished to symbolize it by burning the hand that had held the pen.

"In this way Cranmer dramatized belated obedience to our Lord's words about one's right eye or right hand: 'If your right hand makes you stumble, cut it off.' Jesus wished to make the point that if a man's eye or hand is an uncontrollable instrument of unrighteousness, he is better off without it. Self-mutilation is preferable to the loss of one's soul.

"Hands don't actually sin, of course. Cranmer's hand was no more guilty of sin than are the five fingers of a pickpocket. Thieving is born in the heart, not the hand. Hands and eyes are merely servants, either of sin—which puts them to evil uses—or of God, who uses them for noble purposes.

"Thomas Cranmer's last act was only a gesture. He knew better than most that it was his heart, not his hand, that compelled him to sign the articles of recantation. Fear of the stake, a momentary lapse of courage—it was this or similar motives that prompted the recanting which he later regretted. His hand merely obeyed his fearful heart. But an armless man could not have signed the articles, and if Cranmer had cut his hand off—figuratively speaking, of course—he would not have signed. And so he burned his hand, a belated putting to death of a treacherous member of his body.

"The lesson for us, of course, is to get our hearts under control, molded and shaped by the Word of God, and then, like Paul, to beat our bodies or take whatever steps may be necessary to keep them from betraying us. Let them be our servants, not our masters" (C. Donald Cole, "The Archbishop Burns His Hand"; Moody Bible Institute, Radio Program Schedule).

6

Stand by Your Word!

Truth to Apply: Having taken God's name to myself, I must remember that swearing or breaking a promise involves His reputation, too!

Key Verse: Do not swear at all . . . (Mt. 5:34b).

Our society cannot be proud of its misuse of the name of God. One of the most widespread sins is the employment of sulphurous curse words by men and women in all walks of life. Venture into any public gathering, and after a few minutes you will have heard a full range of cliche-ridden profanities. How can you have a Christian witness in such an environment without being judgmental? How do you handle it at your own place of employment?

Neither Jesus' followers, nor the Pharisees who opposed Him, were inclined to be vulgar of speech or irreverent with God's name. So holy was God's name to them that they did not speak it; instead, they simply referred to "the Name." It seems very unlikely therefore that Jesus is referring here to what we commonly, and rightly, reject as "swearing," or "taking the Lord's name in vain." (You may get a fair idea what the Old Testament Law said—and how this came to be abused in spirit while kept in letter—as well as Jesus' critique, by examining Lev. 19:11, 12; Num. 30:2; Deut. 23:21-23; Mt. 23:16-22; along with Mt. 5:33-37.)

Clearly, the phrase "to the Lord" had been used to create a loophole in the Law: only if you vowed "to the Lord" were you bound to your vow. But Jesus goes to the heart of the matter, cutting through the legalistic red tape: we must be persons who stand by our word. Because we are identified with God, all we do or promise, whether sworn to or not, reflects upon Him. Any failure to keep our word, any infidelity to agreements, profanes His name. To sing hymns of praise, recite prayers or Scriptures, and then leave a church service in order to sin is a violation of the Third Commandment. We take God's name in vain when we only pretend to serve the Lord with heart, strength, and mind. G. Campbell Morgan says, "The form in which this Third commandment is broken most completely, most awfully, most terribly is by perpetually making use of the name of the Lord, while the life does not square with the profession that is made" (G. Campbell Morgan, *The Ten Commandments*).

In simple words, Jesus was blasting hypocrisy and insincerity. (Compare Mt. 23:16-22.) In the Old Testament, the Hebrew for hypocrite is *chaneph;* the root meaning is "polluted" or "profane." The godless person who pollutes, profanes, defiles, and corrupts what is sacred is the hypocrite.

The prophet Isaiah declared that the hypocrite blocks the Lord's hand of mercy (Isa. 9:17). This disease spread through God's chosen people. The vile person practices this pollution (Isa. 32:6). The Lord's might will cause hypocrites to turn fearful (Isa. 33:14). They will not come before God (Job 13:16). The hypocrite will one day lose his hope (Job 27:8). The hypocrite destroys others (Prov. 11:9).

In the New Testament, the Greek word for hypocrite is *hupokrites,* meaning "a play actor," or "a pretender." The noun is related to the verb "to pretend or make believe." Hypocrisy is playing a part and putting on a show. It's wearing a mask and posing as something one really is not.

Jesus warned His disciples about those who play at loving and serving God (Lk. 12:1). Every Christian has to be on guard to keep from profaning the Lord's name by only pretending to obey Him, or by making promises without intending to keep them.

Light on the Text

5:33   Jesus gave His interpretation of the Third Commandment in Matthew 5:33-37. In the first century some Jewish leaders were masters of evasion. They made tricky distinctions between oaths that were binding and ones that were not. (See also Mt. 23:16-22.) They thought they could avoid making an oath binding by not using God's name in it. That meant a person could swear by Heaven, or by Jerusalem, or even one's own head, and feel free to violate the contract agreed to. The idea was that if God's name was used He became a partner to the transaction.

Jesus taught that God is present anytime one enters into a binding agreement. There is nothing in the world that does not belong to God, so it does not matter whether God is named. He is a witness to every transaction.

Reverence for the Name Above All Names

In Bible times, to use another's name meant that you might claim that person's fellowship, help, and service. Jacob, while wrestling with the angel, pleaded, "Please tell me your name" (Gen. 32:29). He was certain that knowledge of the heavenly stranger's name would empower him to deal with the angel on an equal basis. The devotees of heathen religions came to feel that the mere use of their deity's name would produce desired results. On Mt. Carmel, the priests of Baal cut themselves with knives and cried, "O Baal, answer!" (I Ki. 18:26). They thought the repetition of his name would compel him to answer by fire.

God revealed His name to His people. He gave His name, not in order that His followers should have power over Him, but that they might call on Him for help in time of need. His people also enjoy the privilege of that name for fellowship and the intimate experiences of worship. God gave us His name to be used boldly, freely, reverently.

**5:34,
35**
It is a characteristic of ancient Hebrew that when extremes are cited, as in "Heaven and earth," it is intended that everything is included—as when we say, "from soup to nuts," or "from a to z." Through swearing by something which is not God or His name, some people thought to set aside a part of life over which God's rule and oversight did not extend—a loophole. But there is no such area—as Jesus' list of "things not to swear by" attests. The heavens were a favorite entity to swear by because they were considered to be changeless.

**5:36,
37**
So do not swear at all. Simply say yes or no. To multiply categories of truth and obligation beyond yes or no multiplies the possibilities for evil.

It is probably all right for Christians to take oaths in courts of law (in Acts and the Epistles, Paul called on God to witness that he was speaking the truth). But oath taking must be restricted to serious rather than trivial matters. In all cases the name of God should be spoken with honor and respect. Beware of easy familiarity with the Person before whom archangels bow.

The Puritan Perspective

How does a person disobey the Third Commandment? Listen to some answers to this question based on statements by Thomas Watson, 17th-century Puritan, in his book, *A Body of Divinity:*

1. This command is disobeyed when men speak lightly of the Lord's name. That glorious, fearful name is to be feared and given all due reverence.

In our times, many become too familiar with divine names, speaking almost flippantly of the Father, the Savior, or the Spirit. God is always to be approached as a King and Sovereign.

2. The Commandment is broken if God's name is professed by persons who live contrary to His will. The tongue says one thing, the life another. Paul the apostle wrote about people who "claim to know God, but by their actions they deny him" (Titus 1:16).

3. The Lord's name is taken in vain when profane men meddle with His Word. Some scorn God's Word. They speak of the Lord with no reverence.

Others play with the Scripture and even make jokes about it.

Some use the Bible to excuse their sin. Covetousness may be covered over by quoting Exodus 20:9 and I Timothy 5:8. This shows no sincere homage paid the Lord.

4. When men strain their wits to wrest the Word to such a sense as pleases them, they profane God's Word, and take His name in vain.

5. Swearing dishonors God's name. To curse with the name of God is to transgress the Third Commandment. Jesus condemned the use of the Lord's name in a trifling manner to verify what is said. Forswearing is perjury. It shows no reverence toward God. "Ye shall not swear by my name falsely, neither shalt thou profane the name of thy God: I am the Lord" (Lev. 19:12, KJV).

For Discussion

1. Are you a man or woman of your word? If you say you will do something, can it be relied on?

2. Do you have an unpaid loan, or other contract you ignore? Is there an agreement or contract you've signed or are otherwise committed to, which you are keeping only in letter but not in spirit?

3. It has been said that the practical atheism of professing Christians—living as if there were no God, or as if He did not see or care—is responsible for much of the theoretical or dogmatic atheism of unbelievers. What is your opinion?

Window on the Word

Yes, or No?

Graham Scroggie, the Bible expositor, had concluded a service and was about to leave the British Gospel Hall. As he walked to the back of the building, he noticed a young woman still seated in one of the pews. He went over to her and asked, "Would you like to speak with me?"

"Yes," she replied. Then she told Scroggie how the message had challenged her to make a vital decision. She realized the need of choosing between making Christ her Lord or continuing to give first place in her life to someone else.

Scroggie did not offer much advice, for she understood the issues involved and knew what she must do. He did call her attention to a passage in Acts. Peter was on a rooftop when he saw the sheet let down from Heaven. The voice said, "Rise, Peter; kill, and eat" (Acts 10:13).

Peter said, "Not so, Lord; for I have never eaten any thing that is common or unclean." Graham Scroggie pointed to those three words, "Not so, Lord," and showed the young woman that she could not have it both ways. "Either your decision is, 'No, not so,' or it will be, 'Yes, Lord,' " said the teacher.

He left her alone but stayed in the building because the young woman remained in the pew. After a time he saw that her head was bowed in prayer. He slipped up the aisle and glanced at her open Bible. He noticed that with her pencil she had stroked out the words "Not so" and had left "Lord" only.

(Reported in *Keswick Week,* 1971; Marshall, Morgan and Scott.)

7

No More Revenge

Truth to Apply: My behavior is to be determined not by how others treat me, but by the standard of God's righteousness and mercy.

Key Verse: Love your enemies and pray for those who persecute you . . . (Mt. 5:44).

A famous politician recently said that "When voters step into the booth to pull that lever, their question is, 'What have you done for me *lately*?' "

We smile at this, but it touches on the seemingly uncontrollable desire we have to govern all the actions of our lives in light of our own self-interest. Though this drive is concealed when unopposed, it flares up and ruthlessly tries to rule us when our rights are challenged. This challenge may come when we are cheated, ignored, criticized, or placed under the authority of someone else. When was the last time you felt it in your own life? How did you handle it?

At this point in the study, let's take a moment to remind ourselves of the context within which we are working. Matthew writes his portrait of Christ in alternate layers, first of narrative and then of teaching material. The Sermon on the Mount, Matthew 5—7, is the first layer of formal teaching.

The Sermon begins with the Beatitudes, which describe what a person can become in character under the influence of God's grace (5:3-12). Christ then explains (in 5:13-16) how we should relate to those around us. The rest of the Sermon centers on developing the meaning of righteous living. Naturally, this first has to deal with the Law, since, to those who lived in the first century, the Law was the fullest explanation of God's inner character. Therefore, the rest of Matthew 5 examines this, first correcting Pharisaic interpretations of the Law, and then enlarging on its true meaning. Matthew 6 shows the nature of fellowship with God, again in contrast to Pharisaic teaching. Matthew 7 describes true righteousness as it views itself and others.

In this lesson we will examine two "you-have-heard" statements (5:38-42 and 5:43-48) because they are closely related, and because they have a common motivation: to be perfect as our Heavenly Father is perfect (5:48).

The theme uniting the two passages and uniting the behavior of Christians with that of their Father is: Let your behavior be determined by the example of your Father, not by reaction or overreaction to those who abuse you. Give, and do not refuse; love, do not hate.

Light on the Text

5:38   This statement is found in Exodus 21:24, Leviticus 24:20, and Deuteronomy 19:21. As in Christ's earlier references to divorce and oath taking, this command is not designed to stimulate revenge, but to prevent overreaction—to prevent Lamech's response in Genesis

4:23: "I have killed a man for wounding me." We are inclined to hit back when someone offends us, and our emotions often carry us into vengeance.

This element of the Mosaic Law was addressed not to private citizens, but to the judges. Thus it was not meant to authorize private vendettas, but to provide fair legal processes.

This is a much-disputed text in the age-old debate on pacifism and the use of force in the control of evil. We will not try to resolve that question here. From any perspective it is clear Jesus is here speaking against vengeance and retaliation. How this applies to states and their military and police actions is an important question. But for this discussion it may be helpful to think of Jesus as a master householder (Mt. 20:1, KJV) addressing His servants concerning acceptable behavior within the household—ie., the Kingdom. Keeping this in mind we will be able to discover what Jesus is saying.

5:39	The Greek indicates a backhanded blow to the right cheek, which, according to the law, merited twice the fine imposed for an openhanded slap to the left cheek. Jesus emphasizes the insult and yet forbids retaliation.
5:40	The "tunic" was the undergarment; the "cloak" was the outer garment, which, according to Law (Ex. 22:25, 26; Deut. 24:12, 13), could under no circumstances be taken from its owner, not even for a debt owed.
5:41	According to Roman law, a soldier could command a person to carry his pack one mile—but not two. It was a legal right of the soldier. Hence, our expression "to go the extra mile," to go beyond what was already a much-resented duty.
5:42	Here Jesus is simply reiterating Old Testament Law (see Deut. 15:7, 8). It may be that by dropping "your brother," and simply saying, "give to the one who asks you," Jesus is universalizing what the Pharisees had limited to their relatives or to other Jews only.
5:43	Nowhere does the Old Testament combine the command to love with a command to hate. However, the

imprecatory psalms might be thought to approach it (Ps. 69: 23-28, for instance). One explanation of this is that David is here acting in an official capacity, not simply a personal one, and is concerned that the Law and dignity of God be upheld, and that His justice rule the earth.

5:44-46 The theme sentence of the previous passage was negative: "resist not evil." The theme of this paragraph (vss. 43-48) is "love your enemies," the positive side of the same coin. Jesus here uses the strongest of several Greek words for "love": *agape*. This is not merely affection, nor even brotherly love, and certainly not sexual love. This is unselfish love—willing goodwill to another. It is clear from verse 46 that the love meant here is not assured of being returned—as between lovers, or friends and family—but love toward those who do not love us.

5:45-47 The motive of such unselfish love is that we may act like children of our Father in Heaven, manifesting a likeness to Him, following His generous, openhanded example toward the evil and the good, the just and the unjust.

Some have been offended by Matthew's emphasis on "reward" (Mt. 5:12, 46; 6:1, 4, 5, 16, 18). Why be concerned for a "reward"? Why not do good for its own sake? The original word itself provides a clue. Almost everywhere else in Matthew it is translated "pay" or "wages." Your Father in Heaven, a master householder, is asking you to do something which is not satisfying in and of itself—such as returning kindness for insult. So it is appropriate that the one who has commissioned you to this hard work should reimburse you for this labor. "If you love only those who love you, what reward will you get?" The "reward" or "pay," in other words, is a payment in knowledge of the persecution you will undoubtedly endure because of what you have been commanded to do. What you have and what you receive are not the effect of your love or your labor, but a gift from your Father. He is the one for whom you live and work; you are to get your "reward" or "pay" from Him.

5:48 In what sense are we to be "perfect" as our Heavenly Father is "perfect"? The Greek word suggests completeness, wholeness, full development. It is the same word Paul uses for the fully mature Christian (I Cor. 2:6). In the context of verses 45-47 it suggests we should be perfectly fair. Luke's version of this teaching is: "Be merciful, just as your Father is merciful" (Lk. 6:36). It is along such lines that our maturity as Christians should develop.

A Project for Life Response

Surely the passage calls us to take a stand against the sins that twist our walk with God into selfish, irritable, or violent reactions against others. Our first step, therefore, is to tell Christ that we recognize the extent to which self-centeredness has captivated us. Then we should commit ourselves unreservedly to His ways. Further, ask the Holy Spirit for the power to obey. Then, as sin reemerges, repent and return to the joy of intimate fellowship with God.

Here is a project regarding the bitterness infecting our attitudes toward enemies. Think of a person you regard as your enemy. First, view this enemy as God's tool to alert you to your own self-centeredness. Second, thank God in advance that He will use each act of this enemy to help you grow in Christ. Third, repent for any wrong attitude you see in yourself. Fourth, seek ways of serving your enemy—pray for him or her. The focus should be on service, not bitterness.

For Discussion

1. In the teaching of Jesus, the eye-for-an-eye basis of human relations is being replaced by another. What argument or justification for this change does Jesus give?

2. To whom are you now still relating according to "an eye for an eye"? How can you begin to be perfect/merciful in that relationship as your Father would be?

3. In verse 39, is Jesus recommending a "do nothing" response to evil? (See Mt. 18:15-17; Isa. 10:1-4; Mt. 23:13-29.)

4. Besides physical resistance, what alternative ways of responding to evil are there which are not "do nothing" responses? Examine the passage; notice Jesus' commands in particular.

Window on the Word

Down, But Not Out

After Billy Bray, a famous Cornish prizefighter, was converted, a man thought he could hit him without fear. He swung, and connected. Bray, who could easily have knocked him out, simply looked at him and said, "May God forgive you, even as I forgive you." After several days of inner turmoil, the man was converted himself. He saw what God could do in controlling the powerful natural impulses.

8

Keep It Secret!

Truth to Apply: Just as when I am provoked and persecuted, so in my "acts of righteousness" I can live for God rather than for the approval of those around me.

Key Verse: Then your Father, who sees what is done in secret, will reward you (Mt. 6:4b).

Have you ever given someone an anonymous gift? Perhaps you saw someone in financial need and you sent funds with a money order so he or she could not know who did it. Or maybe you left bags of groceries on the steps of a needy family. If you have had this experience, or one similar to it, what kind of feelings did these secret good deeds give you? Did you miss the recognition you could have had if you had "gone public" with your acts of kindness?

With Matthew 6:1ff., Jesus seems to pick up an entirely new theme, seemingly moving on to something unrelated to what He has just been saying in Matthew 5:1-48. The chapter division which has been created here (between 5:48 and 6:1) reinforces this impression. But chapter 6 continues the themes of 5:38-48 in two ways. It is a continuation of Jesus' teaching about loving your neighbor; and it extends the theme of being oriented not to others but to your Father who is in Heaven. Indeed, while 6:1-6, 16-18 tell us what Jesus' disciples' motivation is *not* to be, it does not tell us what it *should* be. This has already been stated in 5:45, "that you may be sons of your Father in heaven."

The structures of the three passages—on almsgiving, prayer, and fasting—are identical. (This makes it clear that verses 7-15 form an extended parenthesis, a separate discussion on prayer.)

As for the emphasis on reward in this context, it is a recompense that Jesus' disciples may legitimately expect, but it is not here viewed as their motivation. The motivation in 6:1-18 is the same as that given for praying for those who persecute you: "that you may be sons of your Father in heaven."

Light on the Text

6:1 Here are expressed in brief all the themes of 6:1-6, 16-18: the key phrase being "before men, to be seen by them." It is a truth instinctively recognized by all—that few things so readily corrupt life and behavior as the slavish submission to mere appearance. We recognize it in the insincerity of politicians, and we despise it in ourselves when we know we have acted or spoken not from sincere conviction but merely in order to be seen by and to gain the favor of others.

Jesus warns His followers that they will lose their reward from the Father if they serve Him only to be seen by others. The doctrine of rewards is taught in the New Testament. Those who are evil will receive the reward of God's judgment of everlasting punishment (Rev. 20:11-15). The faithful, saved solely through the grace of God, will have their works scrutinized before Christ's tribunal (Rom. 14:10-12). A person is not saved by works (Eph. 2:8), but one's conduct following profession of Christ as Savior will be reviewed, and appropriate rewards given or withheld (I Cor. 3:10-15).

Christ declared that hypocrisy can show itself in three areas: giving (Mt. 6:2-4), praying (vss. 5-15), and fasting (vss. 16-18).

6:2-4 As we saw previously, the Greek word translated "hypocrite" can mean a "stage player" or "actor," and, given the emphasis in this passage upon doing in order to be seen by others, we should probably understand "hypocrite" in just this sense: one whose concern is not for the thing itself (giving, praying, fasting) but for the appearance before others.

"To be honored by men" is paralleled by "to be seen by men" and "to show men they are fasting." This is the hypocrite's motivation (see Mt. 23:5a), and it is this which guides our understanding of verse 3. We are here enjoined not to keep a neurotic secrecy over our giving (or praying or fasting), but to act for the sake of the deed itself with an audience of one: our Father who sees in secret.

Just as He drove the moral question deeper than mere public and formal legality, so here, concerned with true spirituality, Jesus drives the question of the exercise of spirituality (embodied here by giving, prayer, and fasting) deeper than mere public and formal piety.

What Christ strikes against is giving for the purpose of self-glorification. "Reward" is from a Greek commercial term, designating payment in full. A. B. Bruce observes, "The hypocrite partly does not believe this, partly does not care, so long as he gets the applause of his public."

6:5 Do not get bogged down here, as some have, in debate over the proper posture for prayer—standing, kneeling, sitting. That is not Jesus' concern. He mentions the hypocrites standing in synagogues and on street corners to pray because standing is a very prominent and visible posture, and visibility is what the hypocrite seeks in prayer. In this he or she is very successful—seen by others—and therefore has received the reward. We are not to pray in order to impress others with our "piety." No overt sin could so quickly shut God's ears to our prayers as when we pray in order to be seen and heard by the congregation rather than by Him.

The posture isn't condemned, but the desire to put devotion on public display is. The hypocrites lashed by Christ committed several transgressions in their praying. They petitioned Heaven in order to show off their piety. They were repetitious (see verse 7). The same words would be said over and over again, moving the speaker into a trancelike state. They were formalists. They possessed a beautiful and meaningful liturgy, but could run through it with no feeling or real devotion.

6:6 "Your room." Judging from its use in other contexts (see Mt. 24:26; Lk. 12:3, 24), this word is to be understood as a secluded place, apart from open and public places. It is the opposite of the synagogue and street corner. Again, we must not misunderstand Jesus' point: He is not forbidding public prayer, for He certainly prayed publicly on occasion. He is commanding His disciples not to draw attention to themselves by prayer, but to draw apart as He Himself did (Mk. 1:35).

6:16-18 Note how ludicrous and absurd this hypocritical piety is: "they disfigure their faces to show men they are fasting." The word translated "disfigure" is the same root word translated "to be seen by men" (vs. 5) and "to show men" (vs. 16). Ironically, it means to "make to disappear," "to vanish," and thus yields also the meaning "to deform or disfigure." Just as actors wear makeup, concealing their true faces in order to appear to be something else, so do these hypocrites conceal their true motives when fasting in public.

Delivered from the extraneous burden of maintaining a false appearance of piety, the faithful disciple is free to give alms, pray, and fast according to the purposes for which these actions exist: honor to God and love to neighbor.

For Discussion

1. Why was Jesus so opposed to the practice of "righteousness" for appearance's sake?

2. What form does this hypocritical desire (to be seen and honored by others) take in your life? How is it manifested in the corporate life of your church?

3. Read Matthew 23:25-32. Three times in this passage Jesus calls the Pharisees "hypocrites." Put yourself in their place. Imagine that Jesus had charged you in this way. What in your life, and in the life of your church, could He be referring to?

4. A Biblical prohibition is always the flip side of a positive obligation or command. Prohibition of hoarding is not merely a call to give up material wealth, but a positive command to care for the poor. Likewise with fasting. Read Isaiah 58 and, in light of it, discuss why fasting just for appearance's sake is especially opposed to God's will. If a somber look and a disfigured face is not the sign of true fasting, what is?

Window on the Word

Who Said It?

"The union with Christ provides moral edification, consolation in sorrow, and quiet confidence; a heart open to the love of mankind, all things noble, and all greatness; not for ambition, or desire for fame, but only for love of Christ."

Who made this statement? Were these words uttered by a devout child of God in centuries past? Or by some renowned preacher of the Word?

You may be surprised to learn that the quote was penned by a young man, 17 years old, in a graduation essay, "Union with Christ." You may also be surprised to know that the writer was *Karl Marx, the father of Communism!*

Many who announce their allegiance "with trumpets" later prove to be less than faithful.

9

A Prayer for All Seasons

Truth to Apply: The Lord's Prayer gives me a model for fashioning my attitudes of worship, petition, forgiveness, and dependence on God's power.

Key Verse: Your kingdom come, your will be done on earth as it is in heaven (Mt. 6:10).

This has been called an "age of anxiety." Worry reveals itself in many ways: a high divorce rate, sexual promiscuity, rootlessness, sickness, alcoholism, drug abuse, and retreat into the fantasy world of television.

These and many other signs point to massive fears: fear of complexity; fear of rapid and continual change; fear of the unfamiliar; fear of being depersonalized and impersonalized; fear of economic collapse; fear of deteriorating personal relationships, especially in the family.

Tragically, at a time when fear is perhaps more widespread and deep rooted than ever before, the fallen world largely ignores the only effective antidote to anxiety: putting God and His Kingdom first.

How do you, personally, deal with the temptation to worry?

The larger contextual passage (6:1-15) contains four sections:

1. The first section (vss. 1-4) contains instructions on almsgiving. Jesus declares that we are not to perform good deeds just to be seen by others.

2. Sayings on prayer (vss. 5-8). Here Jesus tells how and how not to pray.

3. The model prayer (vss. 9-13). Although called the "Lord's Prayer," this is not His prayer for Himself, but the prayer given by Him to show His disciples the way to pray.

4. Comments on forgiveness (vss. 14, 15); a summing up of what is said about forgiveness in the Lord's Prayer.

Light on the Text

6:6, 7   The NEB and the NIV have wisely chosen to translate the obscure Greek word *battalogeo,* as "babbling." It should not be understood as prohibiting repetition in prayer (as the KJV's "vain repetition" does), unless by that we mean a thoughtless "heap[ing] up [of] empty phrases" (RSV). Jesus Himself repeated His request in Gethsemane (Mt. 26:44).

6:8   Though we will not be heard, as the pagans think, because of our many words, neither will we be heard by our Father without a request—a request which is strengthened in hope precisely because the Father knows and is inclined to supply the needs of His children (Mt. 6:25-32). "It is . . . natural and legitimate to ask for things of whose need we are conscious; to keep them back would be to erect a barrier between ourselves and God" (T. H. Robinson, *The Gospel of Matthew*).

6:9-13   Each of the two main parts of the prayer contain three petitions—a total of six in all:

First Petition: "Hallowed be your name." The name of God is held in reverence and awe. "May your holy name be honored" (*Today's English Version*). How does God sanctify His name? By condemning sin; by giving humanity love and grace.

Second Petition: "Your kingdom come." The Kingdom is the "rule of God." When God is supreme in a person's heart the Kingdom of God is active there.

Third Petition: "Your will be done." God's will is spoken of in three senses: God's will of purpose; God's will of desire; and God's will of command. In Heaven, the perfect will of God is done, but not on earth.

Fourth Petition: "Give us today our daily bread." Bread was the staff of life. Here is a single petition for earthly need; a recognition of God's care for us as the Sustainer of all life.

Fifth Petition: "Forgive us our debts." Sins are to be recognized as debts; sinners as debtors (Mt. 18:23-25).

Sixth Petition: "Lead us not into temptation." *Phillips' Translation* says: "Keep us clear of temptation." We need God's help in finding strength to meet life's testings. Some interpreters make "deliver us from the evil one" a seventh petition. But it is more properly a second part of the sixth.

6:9, 10   Calling God "Father" helps us to think of Him and recognize Him as a person who is close to us instead of as a distant deity. It helps us to think of ourselves as His children (see Jn. 1:12; Rom. 8:16), speaking our petitions to the one who heads up and has authority over the "family of the redeemed." Notice, too, that we are to pray "Our Father." This suggests a sense of being joined with others when we pray. Thus our prayers are to be personal and even individual, but not to the exclusion of other members of Christ's Body. "'Hallowed be your name' means literally 'Thy name be made holy,' and recalls (by way of contrast) the phrase used by Amos 2:7, 'to profane my holy name'" (Robinson). It is to say, "May all that is done in the world—including the worship and life of your people—bring honor to you as the supreme and holy God."

6:11   Some scholars say this verse should be translated, "Give us today our bread for the morrow." There is some dispute over the word "morrow," which others prefer to translate as "today." In any case, the sense of immediate need (as against anticipated future need) is in the forefront, just as it is in Matthew 6:34.

6:12   Just as the first set of petitions concerns God and His Kingdom, so the second set concerns us and our needs. But this shift from God to us necessarily includes our neighbor and our relation to him or her. It is natural, then, that we find here a petition for forgiveness which is linked to our forgiveness of those who are "in debt" to us. Our spirituality (our relationship to God) is never independent of our social relationships.

6:13   Since the Bible tells us that God does not tempt us with evil (Jas. 1:13), what can this petition possibly mean? John R. W. Stott has a clear and helpful suggestion: "We could paraphrase the whole request as 'Do not allow us so to be led into temptation that it overwhelms us, but rescue us from the evil one. . . . Thus the three petitions Jesus puts upon our lips are beautifully comprehensive. They cover, in principle, all our human need—material (daily bread), spiritual (forgiveness of sins) and moral (deliverance from evil). What we are doing whenever we pray this prayer is to express our dependence upon God in every area of our human life" (John R. W. Stott, *Christian Counter-Culture: The Message of the Sermon on the Mount*).

6:14, 15   These verses are a commentary on verses 12 and 13, and anticipate the parable in Matthew 18:23-35. The axiom stated in the Beatitudes ("Blessed are the merciful") is here developed into an explanation of our relationship with God and neighbor, and, in Matthew 18:21-35, it is illustrated by Jesus' striking and compelling parable.

Think Before You Pray

"There is too much praying without thinking," declares David Mains in a magazine article. "Making proper requests of God demands prior consideration. It is small wonder that so little happens in the area of answered prayer when one considers the lack of intelligent asking."

To combat this, Rev. Mains says he has learned to ask himself six simple questions. These questions can help any Christian develop a more effective prayer life:

1. "What is it I want?" Our prayers should be specific; all too often our incantations indicate a serious lack of decisiveness (see Mt. 6:7).

2. "Can God grant my request?" Of course, there is nothing that He is not able to do. Yet there are certain things God will not do, things contrary to His nature or to His expressed will (see Mt. 6:10; 26:42).

3. "Have I done my part?" Am I asking for something that God expects me to accomplish myself? (see Eph. 3:20).

4. "What is our present relationship?" Is there anything standing between you and the One to whom you are making your request? If so, the problem must be cleared up before going further (see I Jn. 3:21, 22).

5. "Have I considered His interests?" If your supplication is not in God's interest, it stands to reason it is for your own desire alone (see Jas. 4:3).

6. "Do I expect an answer?" This is the most important question—it hinges on one's faith. I must believe in order to receive answers to my prayers (see Mk. 11:24).

In closing this article, Rev. Mains says: "In an exciting way, I believe you will begin to see requests granted regularly as you practice 'thinking before you pray.' " (Reprinted by permission of *Eternity* Magazine, Copyright 1971, Evangelical Ministries, Inc.)

For Discussion

1. What good reason can you see for praying "Our Father in heaven" rather than just "God" or "Lord"? How have you found comfort in being God's "child"?

2. Why is it essential to pray, "Forgive us our debts, as we also have forgiven our debtors"? Where does the idea of restitution fit in?

3. Why pray if God knows what we need before we ask? Share among your group what new things you have learned about prayer and praying. Think of ways to apply these insights to group prayer.

Window on the Word

Some Key Words

Five key words help to give us the meaning of prayer: adoration, confession, thanksgiving, submission, supplication.

Adoration. Worship in prayer is expressed well in Psalm 95:6, "Come, let us bow down in worship, let us kneel before the Lord our Maker."

We think about God; we bow before Him. Then we express adoration with such words as these: "Glory be to the Father, the Son, and the Holy Spirit."

Confession. An excellent prayer of confession is found in Isaiah 6:5: "'Woe to me!' I cried. 'I am ruined! For I am a man of unclean lips, and I live among a people of unclean lips, and my eyes have seen the King, the Lord Almighty.'"

The confessor faces up to his or her own sin, pride, self-will, self-centeredness, and rebellion against God. And in the Model Prayer one rightly prays: "Forgive us our debts, as we forgive our debtors."

Thanksgiving. This is the acknowledgement of God's gifts. The psalmist prayed: "Praise the Lord, O my soul" (Ps. 103: 1, 2). Give thanks for everything: for the Creation, home, family, friends, daily work, recreation, our Lord's life, His ascension, the promise of His coming, the Holy Spirit.

Supplication. This means to entreat for; to ask earnestly and humbly.

Submission. Jesus prayed a prayer of submission when in Gethsemane: "My Father, if it is possible, may this cup be taken from me. Yet not as I will, but as you will" (Mt. 26:39).

Submission means to offer our petitions in Christ's name and Christ's will. Jesus said: "Whatever you ask in my name, I will do it, that the Father may be glorified in the Son; if you ask anything in my name, I will do it" (Jn. 14:13, 14, *RSV*).

10

The Heart and the Wallet

Truth to Apply: Christ calls me to decide between two potential masters in this life: God or money.

Key Verse: Where your treasure is, there your heart will be also (Mt. 6:21).

Our Puritan forebears believed in the value of good hard work. "They that will not sweat on earth shall sweat in hell," said the sixteenth-century divine, Henry Smith. All people were to have a calling, that is, an occupation, and to "walk diligently" in it.

But in place of the Puritans' sense of divine election, many hardworking people have made net worth the measure of self-worth. As Chun King founder Jeno Paulucci told Marilyn Machlowitz, author of *Workaholics: Living with Them, Working with Them* (Addison-Wesley), "My career goal has always been to make money ethically and honestly, not only to make money for the currency value but as a measure of success—just like someone playing golf, his score card is his measure of success in that game. In my game, it is making money." Paulucci, like so many others, is unable to stop working—even when on vacation. He wrote to researcher Machlowitz: "I am now dictating this from Acapulco. I don't even leave the phone. I'm pacing around this pool, wondering what I should do next. I'm writing memos, calling the office, calling New York, calling Chicago. I just can't relax." (Adapted and reprinted by permission of *HIS*, student magazine of InterVarsity Christian Fellowship, ©1984.)

How would you describe the difference between earning a living and serving money? How have you dealt with the money issue in your own life?

From teaching on the "acts of righteousness" of alms, prayer, and fasting, Jesus proceeds, apparently without connection or transition, to warn about greed (vss. 19-24) and about anxiety for material needs (vss. 25-34). But if we have been correct in reading Jesus' teaching (concerning fasting) against the Old Testament background of Isaiah 58, then verses 19-34 follow very naturally from it: the active and positive aspect of fasting is the appropriation of our material wealth for the benefit of the poor. Both greed and excessive concern for the accumulation of wealth stand in the way of seeking first God's righteousness and Kingdom.

In other words, it is not surprising, but quite logical, that Jesus should follow His teachings on alms, prayer, and fasting with teachings on the obstacles to these "acts of righteousness."

When studying the Bible, it is often helpful to use one passage to illuminate another, to provide a fuller, deeper understanding. A passage from the first letter of John helps us interpret Christ's teaching concerning the treasures of earth and the treasures of Heaven. Of course, I John was written after Matthew's Gospel. But its teachings are based upon the words and ideas of Jesus.

"Do not love the world or anything in the world. If anyone loves the world, the love of the Father is not in him. For everything in the world—the cravings of sinful man, the lust of his eyes and the boasting of what he has and does—comes not from the Father but from the world. The world and its desires pass away, but the man who does the will of God lives forever" (I Jn. 2:15-17).

"World" refers to the entire Creation in bondage to sin—the fallen world under the influence of Satan (I Jn. 5:19), but which God loved enough to redeem with the blood of His only begotten Son (Jn. 3:16). Humanity is under control of the fallen, rebellious spirit of this world (Eph. 2:2) until liberation comes through Christ (Gal. 5:1).

Thus, "world" means the same thing as "earth," in the words of Jesus found in Matthew 6:19. Treasures "upon earth" (in the world) are not permanent and are therefore not worth making all important. The rebellious world (earth) is under God's judgment. Eventually it will be destroyed.

A sense that this world is temporary, transient, passing away, is basic to Holy Scripture. The psalmist of Israel said, "You have made my days a mere handbreadth; the span of my years is as nothing before you. Each man's life is but a breath. Man is a mere phantom as he goes to and fro: He bustles about, but only in vain; he heaps up wealth, not knowing who will get it."

Perhaps the clincher is the parable Jesus told concerning the rich fool who got preoccupied with his property and rich harvests. Suddenly, God called him to account. His precious treasures upon earth became valueless.

Light on the Text

6:19   Because houses of that day had walls of mud, burglars could easily break in and steal one's valuable possessions inside.

"Moth" refers to destruction of cloth, or the clothing which is so important to many people. "Rust," affecting things made of metal, symbolizes destruction of property by the natural process of deterioration.

It is the nature of earthly treasure to be radically insecure, passing, undependable. Earthly treasure, you might say, is a risky investment. It could easily leave you facing a heavy loss.

6:20   We are instead to store up treasures in Heaven. "On earth" and "in heaven" are literal locations, but figuratively, they refer to treasure of earthly or heavenly quality or character.

Treasures in Heaven are those values which are treasured in Heaven, i.e., by our Heavenly Father. His values are clear through Jesus' teachings. To give to the poor is to lend to the Lord. Treasures in Heaven are those things which have eternal importance because they are important in God's Kingdom.

6:21   This verse is critical to the whole of Matthew 6:19-34. It is critical to a proper interpretation of this section. It is often read and understood as if Jesus were saying that the intentions and values of our heart, our sincere inner commitment, will determine where our treasure is—as if He were saying that our treasure follows the lead of the heart's allegiance. ("Heart" means the center of a person's total being—the will, the emotions, the personality—the whole self.) But this is not what He is saying. Look closely. First the location of our treasure is ascertained, then, by the location of our treasure—on earth or in Heaven, we may know where the heart is. The heart's true allegiance is indicated by the location of the treasure. The heart is deceitful above all things and will lie about its truest commitments. But what you actually do with your time, money, and energy points infallibly to your heart's true allegiance. What a sobering teaching!

6:22   The Greek word here translated "good" ("sound" in the RSV and "single" in the KJV) is found also in the Greek version of the Old Testament at Proverbs 11:24-26; I Chronicles 29:17; and in the New Testament at Romans 12:8; II Corinthians 8:2; 9:11, 13; James 1:5; where it always means "generous." (Though, in light of verse 24, it may also mean "undivided commitment.")

  This verse reflects the ancient belief that the eye was like a window, through which light entered and affected the whole body.

6:23   In this verse we find the opposite member to the good eye of verse 22: a bad eye, or evil eye. This phrase may simply refer to a blind eye which admits no light—hence, the body is full of darkness. But we are still left trying to understand what that means.

  It is helpful to know that this exact phrase—literally "your evil eye"—occurs also in Matthew 20:15 and Mark 7:22. In Matthew 20:15 it is paraphrased, "are you envious?" (in the KJV it is, "is your eye evil?") and in Mark 7:22 it is paraphrased, "envy" (NIV, KJV: "an evil eye"). Judging from these contexts, it appears to have been a figure of speech meaning stinginess toward others. Alan Hugh McNeile writes that Matthew "seems, therefore, to have interpreted it of a right and wrong spirit with regard to earthly possessions" (*The Gospel According to St. Matthew*).

6:24 The word "serve" is from the Greek word for "slave." It means to serve as a slave. Hence the impossibility of serving two masters. The reason for this impossibility is spelled out in the next sentence: though a slave may occasionally obey a command of one master and later a command of another, his or her love, devotion, and allegiance are, nevertheless, owed to one or the other (or neither?), but not to both simultaneously.

Verse 24 is set up like a logical argument. The major premise is "No one can serve two masters." The minor premise is twofold and part of it is implicit: serving means giving absolute and exclusive obedience. Therefore (the conclusion): "You cannot serve God and Money."

For Discussion

1. "Treasure" is not money and financial investments alone. What other forms of treasure do we have? What does it mean to put these treasures where moth and rust cannot harm them and thieves cannot steal them?

2. Do you agree that "where your treasure is, there your heart will be also"? What would an analysis of your personal, family, and church budgets indicate about where your treasure and your heart are?

3. What would a breakdown of our local, state, and national budgets tell us about where our society's heart is?

Window on the Word

Grasping Hands

When workers were digging to lay a foundation for a new building outside the city of Pompeii, they discovered another victim of that disastrous volcanic explosion from Vesuvius. They found the body of a woman who must have been fleeing the eruption but got caught in the rain of hot ashes. What was so strange about this discovery was the woman's hands were filled with jewels. The hands clutched gems preserved in excellent condition: rings, necklaces, amulets, bracelets, and an especially stunning pair of earrings (pearls set in gold). Someone dead grasping onto earth's treasures!

Never Own Anything

"I do not mean by this that you cannot have things. I mean that you ought to get delivered from the sense of possessing them. This sense of possessing is what hinders us. All babies are born with their fists clenched, and it seems to me it means 'This is mine!' One of the first things they say is 'mine' in an angry voice. That sense of 'This is mine' is a very injurious thing to the spirit. If you can get rid of it so that you have no feeling of possessing anything, then will come a great sense of freedom and liberty into your life." (A. W. Tozer, in "Five Vows for Spiritual Power," Christian Publications, Inc.)

11

A Life Without Worry

Truth to Apply: Anxiety about life distorts my values and is an obstacle to spiritual growth.

Key Verse: Do not worry about tomorrow, for tomorrow will worry about itself. Each day has enough trouble of its own (Mt. 6:34).

Every now and then, we ask ourselves, "Do I have enough? Some people around here seem more comfortable with some of the extras they have. Have I done all I can to provide for tomorrow?"

Sometimes that feeling is merely the desire, prudent and commonplace, to double-check our preparations for present and future family needs—food, clothing for the changing seasons, maintenance of the car, and so on. At other times, however, we look at what others own and feel our possessions pale by comparison. We find ourselves wanting what we don't have—and usually don't need. This can make us tough to live with, if not downright unpleasant.

And doesn't that frustration bring with it, during certain turns of our minds, the temptation to worry? We may even feel the urge to steal! If, by being anxious about tomorrow's needs today, we fail to live faithfully in the present, then we will never live faithfully at all, but always only be anxious about tomorrow—and envious of what is not within our present reach.

What does it mean, for you, to live one day at a time without worry or envy?

Jesus had been cautioning against hypocrisy and the attempt to be double minded. The heart is where the treasure is; true loyalty can only go to one master; "You cannot serve both God and Money"; "Therefore . . . do not worry about your life . . . ."

Regarding the Sermon on the Mount, Albert Barnes has observed: "In all languages there is not a discourse to be found that can be compared with it for purity, and truth, and beauty, and dignity. Were there no other evidence of the divine mission of Christ, this alone would be sufficient to prove that He was sent from God."

Light on the Text

6:25   Because earthly treasures are ephemeral and elusive, because if your eye is stingy your whole self will be dark, because you can truly serve only one master, therefore do not be preoccupied continually with food and clothing. Food and clothes are fine servants, but bad masters.

6:26, 27   The phrase "birds of the air" is from Genesis 1:26 (and its commentary, Ps. 104:12), reminding us of the Creator, among whose creatures we are. The Greek word here translated "look" means to look attentively, to gaze earnestly upon something. The KJV is better: "Behold the fowls of the air." The parallel word in verse 28 has a similar meaning: consider, observe carefully and thoroughly. Together they suggest an approach opposite to continual worry and preoccupation: Do not worry, instead reflect on God's care for His creatures. To worry does nothing but steal joy from daily living.

6:28   The word for "worry" here means to be wearied or spent with labor, faint from weariness. It is the same word Jesus uses in Matthew 11:28—"Come to me, all you who are weary . . . ." Here is the easy yoke and the light

burden of Jesus' way! Be always considering your
Father's loving care.

6:29 See the modesty and simplicity of our Lord, who prefers
the unpretentious and plain beauty of a flower or a
blade of grass to the luxurious and ultimately
unsatisfying splendor of Solomon!

6:30 Here is a double-edged proverb. Our lives are as fleeting
as the grass (see Ps. 90: 5, 6; Is. 40:6).

6:30-32 Therefore, do not waste your brief life with worry over
necessary but fleeting things, which your Father knows
you need.

6:33 Balanced against all the prohibitions of the preceding
verses, here is the single positive command. The word
"seek" has the same root meaning as in "the pagans run
after all these things." It means to pursue, to endeavor to
obtain. In the face of your basic daily needs, and despite
the threat even of economic privation due to persecution
for righteousness' sake, go ahead, trust God your Father,
and seek first His Kingdom and His righteousness.

6:34 We all live between Paul's statement, "He who will not
work, let him not eat" and Jesus' statement, "Be not
anxious about tomorrow." One can be unfaithful and
presumptuous in either direction. We live and plan
toward secure and comfortable retirements; we have
large insurance policies; some Christians have enormous
stockpiles of food. To consider future needs is only
prudent. Is Jesus forbidding this?

This much is clear: the Kingdom must be the first
priority: we may give our hearts and devotion to no
other god, but only to the Lord; and we must not let
"prudence" toward tomorrow make our eye stingy
toward our brothers and sisters today.

For Discussion

1. It is clear that Jesus seeks to remove obstacles to our
entering the Kingdom. Why would anxiety about

food/clothing/tomorrow be an obstacle? What forms might this anxiety take? What is the basic issue here?

2. What is "enough"? Do you think I Timothy 6:6-8 might be an apt commentary on Matthew 6:25-34?

3. What are the emotional and spiritual consequences of worry in your own life?

Window on the Word

Willing to Be Made Willing

In *The Power of a Surrendered Life* (Moody Press), J. Wilbur Chapman, the famous evangelist who preceded Billy Sunday, recounted:

"For five years I had struggled against what I believed was God's plan for my life, but to walk in the way He had marked out was to change all the plans of my student life and my early ministerial career; it was to give up the things I had worked for years to obtain; and the fact is, I was unwilling to do it.

The sacrifice was too great in my estimation, and the returns would be too small. No words can describe the unrest that filled my soul. At last one day I was sitting in my home in the country, reading the account of Mr. Meyer's address at the Northfield Conference, when my eye lighted upon this expression: "'If you are not willing to forsake everything for God, then are you ready to say, "I am willing to be made willing"?'

"That seems a very simple sentence when put into words, but it was for me a star of hope in what was midnight darkness. I felt that I could say that, and upon my knees I whispered: 'I am willing to be made willing.'

"In less time than I am taking to write it, God lifted the cloud that had been before me for years. He removed the mountain over which it seemed impossible for me to pass, and suddenly the way became bright. . . ."

12

To Judge, or Not To Judge?

Truth to Apply: Christ calls me to a consistent Christian life-style in which I avoid comparing myself with the shortcomings of others.

Key Verse: Do not judge, or you too will be judged (Mt. 7:1).

Christians today, both clergy and laity, are angry with their churches. God promises to forgive His people, but most Christians are prepared only to judge. When the dinner table conversation drifts to the subject of the church, the children have learned to brace themselves to hear heated words.

One large denomination, which has experienced almost a 35 percent drop in giving to denominational causes, now finds itself in a virtual battleground between "leaders" and "followers," both sides hurling countercharges.

And the world? It looks on with amusement and cynicism. As one of the Church Fathers wrote, "For when the heathen hear God's oracles on our lips they marvel at their beauty and greatness. But . . . . When they see that we fail to love not only those who hate us, but even those who love us, then they mock at us and scoff the Name" *(II Clement).*

Clearly, the local church is a sphere in which Christ's teaching on judgment and forgiveness can be most relevant. How do the members of your church deal with the matter of judgmental attitudes?

To understand properly the New Testament's teaching about judgment and forgiveness, we must know why the Pharisees were so judgmental, why Jesus opposed their judgments, and why the first-century Church remembered His teaching.

First, why were the Pharisees so prone to be critical? We must see the answer against the backdrop of the persecution and oppression the Jews had experienced for centuries at the hands of the Gentiles.

Egypt had enslaved the Hebrews; in the eighth century B.C. the Assyrians had harassed them; the sixth-century Babylonians robbed them and destroyed the Temple; throughout the Restoration the Samaritans persecuted them; and a later Greek dynasty declared their religion illegal. Quite naturally, the Jews grew touchy, and one must sympathize with their complaints. Hear this cry from the Psalms: "Rescue me, O Lord, from evil men; protect me from men of violence. . . . I know that the Lord secures justice for the poor and upholds the cause of the needy" (Ps. 140:1, 12).

Suffering for being a distinct people led some Jews to overemphasize their unique relation to God and especially the value of God's gift of the Law. As a result, those who tried to adhere strictly to the Law began to see those Jews who did not as being almost as bad as the Gentiles. In other words, those who did not follow the proper rules became objects of scorn.

Why, then, did Jesus oppose the Pharisees' judgments? Because the Pharisees fell prey to the great danger that exists in being right. They became proud. They passed from righteousness to self-righteousness, from indignation to hatred.

Around the end of the first century A.D. the rabbis even constructed the following "test" benediction (designed to exclude heretics) which every synagogue worshiper repeated: "For the renegades let there be no hope, and may the arrrogant kingdom soon be rooted out in our days, and the Nazarenes . . . perish as in a moment and be blotted out from the book of life." And then the final, almost unbelievably hypocritical, sentence:

"Blessed art thou, O Lord, who humblest the arrogant" (From C. K. Barrett's *The New Testament Background*). Blessed indeed! It is no wonder Jesus commended the meek but chastised the Pharisees.

But now to the third question: why did the New Testament writers remember and record Jesus' teaching about the spirit of judgment? To be sure, the Gospels are not mere diaries or record books. They are first-century handbooks, written to be used in worship, teaching, and proclaiming the Gospel to the world. For very practical reasons they included the saying of Jesus about judgment and forgiveness, namely, to oppose the spirit of judgment among Christians. Jesus addressed His words to the Jews who lived around A.D. 30, but the evangelists recalled and recorded His words for the benefit of the Christians who lived around A.D. 60-70. The early church, we must remember, was not idyllic. "There arose a murmuring of the Grecians against the Hebrews" (Acts 6:1, KJV); with the Christian Judaizers "Paul and Barnabas had no small dissension and disputation" (Acts 15:2, KJV); later, between Paul and Barnabas "there arose a sharp contention" (Acts 15:39, RSV); in Antioch, Paul grew angry with Peter's conduct and "opposed him to his face, because he was in the wrong" (Gal. 2:11); to Corinth, Paul wrote, "My brothers, some . . . have informed me that there are quarrels among you" (I Cor. 1:11); and in the Epistle to the Romans (written about A.D. 57), Paul counseled, "Therefore let us stop passing judgment on one another" (Rom. 14:13). Yes, the gospel writers had excellent reasons for remembering the sayings of Jesus about the spirit of judgment and forgiveness.

The whole tone of this passage is embodied in the prohibition, "Judge not" and the corresponding command, "Ask." Both commands must be heard in the context of a gracious Heavenly Father, the master householder who sends rain on the just and the unjust (5:45), and provides for the needs of each of His creatures (6:25-33). In view of this master, who are we to judge another's servant? And since we live only by the grace of this master, we are not in a position to demand anything—not a fastidious righteousness from others, or anything from God; we may only give and ask.

Light on the Text

7:1, 2 There is some question whether the judgment threatened to those who judge is the final judgment by God, or the immediate judgment in kind by one's peers. The Greek word for "judge" can be and is used throughout the New Testament for both. Here it may include both senses. Many are inclined to emphasize the human judgment because of the context: a critical attack is generally answered by a judging rejoinder.

The sense of "judge" here seems to be: "Do not condemn." To judge in the sense of "discerning" is not forbidden, for discernment is assumed in verse 6.

Sir Thomas More, Lord Chancellor of England, having been condemned to death on false grounds, addressed his judges thus: "More have I not to say, my lords, but that Saint Paul held the clothes of those who stoned Stephen to death, and as they are now both saints in heaven, and shall continue there friends forever; so I verily trust, and shall most heartily pray, that though your lordships have now here on earth been judges to my condemnation, we may nevertheless hereafter cheerfully meet in heaven in everlasting salvation."

7:3-5 Here again Jesus makes His point with a bit of humorous hyperbole. The image of someone presuming to be concerned about a speck in another's eye, while one's own eye has a log jammed in it, is both outrageous and funny. Picture it!

The word translated "speck" means any particle, as of chaff, a small splinter, or a dust mote. "Plank" means a spar or beam of timber. Notice (vs. 5) that Jesus does not prohibit helping with the speck in another's eye; what is prohibited is the presumption to do this without dealing with the even greater obstacle to one's own vision. No double standards: use one measure or scale—for what you give and for what you receive. (Possibly the best commentary on this passage is Paul's in Rom. 14:10-18.)

7:6 This obscure verse is possibly a corollary to verses 1-5. Even if you have cleared your own eye and have a sincere and needed word for your brother or sister, he or she may—if a dog, a fool—not be able to hear it. In which case it may be better to keep your pearl of wisdom. (See Prov. 9:7, 8.)

The *Didache* (an early collection of church teachings after the apostles) indicates how certain leaders in the early church understood this passage: "But let none eat or drink of your Eucharist except those who have been baptized in the Lord's Name. For concerning this also did the Lord say, 'Give not that which is holy to the dogs.'"

7:7-11 The passives (be given you, be opened to you) strongly hint that, as we have seen before in the Sermon, we can never demand, nor can we acquire anything by our own effort alone. We are in the vulnerable position of having to ask, seek, knock. This is a frightening place to be: if we ask someone's forgiveness, they may refuse it; if we ask for compassion, it too, may be withheld; if we seek acceptance, we may be rejected. To ask, seek, knock—as over against grasping and demanding—requires great faith and trust. Notice the episodes in Matthew's Gospel when people came to ask something of Jesus: 8:1-4, 5-13; 9:27-31; 15:21-28. Jesus assures us that we will receive if we ask of our Father.

7:12 With verse 12 we are back to the equal measure of verse 2: if you would receive generously, give generously. But this sums up Jesus' teaching on mercy (5:7, 43-48), as indeed it should, for it is a summation of all of Jesus' teaching on the Law. The mention of Law and Prophets reminds us of the opening passage of this lecture on Law, 5:17-20.

But notice that verse 12 (the "Golden Rule") is not a promise that others will return the favor. The argument for this rule is not the pragmatic one that others will do to you what you do to them. Rather, the rule is recommended because "this is the Law and the Prophets" behind which is the authority of the Father, who is perfect in that He makes His sun rise on the evil and the good. The argument for the Golden Rule is that it exemplifies the master householder's behavior, which is to be emulated by all His servants.

For Discussion

1. A common way to cheat in business in the past was the use of two scales: one for what you receive, and another, different scale for what you give. Can you see ways that you measure yourself by one standard and others by another?

2. Does "judge not" mean to never exercise our critical or discriminating faculties? Why or why not?

3. Ask, seek, and knock seem to be introduced rather suddenly. For what, do you suppose, are we to ask, seek, and knock?

Window on the Word

Forgive Yourself

Christians are fond of saying, "Hate the sin, but love the sinner," but they rarely do this to themselves. They may try to forgive others, but they despair of personal forgiveness. Day after day they carry the weight of self-judgment; year after year they blame themselves for their sins. Karl Menninger tells this true story: "On a sunny day in September, 1972, a stern-faced, plainly dressed man could be seen standing still on a street corner in the busy Chicago Loop. As pedestrians hurried by on their way to lunch or business, he would solemnly lift his right arm, and pointing to the person nearest him, intone loudly the single word 'GUILTY!' . . . The effect . . . on the passing strangers was extraordinary, almost eerie. . . . One man, turning to another . . . exclaimed: 'But how did *he* know?' " (Karl Menninger, *Whatever Became of Sin?* Hawthorn.)

13

The False and Foolish

Truth to Apply: Christ's teachings remind me that the life of discipleship is a challenge requiring discernment, wisdom, and perseverance.

Key Verse: Enter through the narrow gate. For wide is the gate and broad is the road that leads to destruction, and many enter through it (Mt. 7:13).

Caveat emptor (Latin for "let the buyer beware") has long been a rule of practice in the marketplace. Test-drive that car before you buy it, we are told. Squeeze that grapefruit; recline on that mattress; inspect that house; run that vacuum sweeper; read up on that aluminum siding. And so we do. We have become fastidiously consumer conscious.

But what about the weightier things of life—the principles we believe in, the teachers we listen to, the standards we follow, the convictions we hold? Do we run these through the same kind of testing? Do we care as much about our Christianity as we do about our cauliflower?

Jesus often used exaggerated contrasts in His teaching, a very effective way of putting across points. This method, known as hyperbole, shows up frequently in the Sermon on the Mount, particularly in the last segment (Mt. 7).

For example, hypocrites, He says, are those who are so busy pointing out the specks in others' eyes that they fail to see the logs in their own. He cautions against casting pearls before swine and giving holy things to dogs. He paints an outlandishly bad picture of fathers (who would give a child a stone instead of bread, or a serpent instead of a fish) in order to illustrate God's surpassing fatherly goodness. Christ seems to delight in stretching our minds and our hearts to the limits.

The closing portion of the Sermon on the Mount (this lesson) contains several examples of hyperbole. Jesus likens false prophets to wolves in sheep's clothing—at face value, a rather ludicrous sight; yet to the agrarian people of Jesus' day, a vivid and memorable comparison.

He asks if "men gather grapes of thorns, or figs of thistles." Obviously, they do not. (They may be fooled by some grapelike or figlike vegetation—but it will be just that: foolery.)

He points out the sad consequences awaiting thousands who profess discipleship yet don't even know Him.

Finally, He tells how two men building two similar houses can have opposite results when disaster strikes. Totally opposite foundations—rock and sand—spell the difference.

We can miss much of the strength and energy of the sayings of Jesus if we overlook these powerful techniques—exaggeration and vivid contrast. They were effective tools throughout Christ's teaching ministry.

Among the many chorales written on the Gospel texts by J. S. Bach, there is one based on Matthew 7:21-23. Though some people find this Bible passage frightening and disturbing, they can be comforted and edified by the music Bach wrote for it. The music, surprisingly, is joyous and full of hope, not somber and threatening, as we might have written it. Bach had apparently seen in this passage not merely the debunking of all our inadequate and sinful works and all our verbal claims and posturings, but also a deep and reassuring foundation of hope and joy: the evangelical message that God has accomplished by grace what human effort could not.

It is in this spirit that we should come to the final passages of the Sermon on the Mount and, as it happens, to the final study in our series.

Jesus has summed up the Law and Prophets in 7:12, bringing to a close His direct teachings about the Law. Now (vss. 13ff) begins His exhortation to His disciples: (1) enter the narrow gate; (2) beware of false prophets; and (3) do the will of My Father, that is, do My words (vs. 24).

Light on the Text

7:13, 14   At the outset of His exhortation, like Joshua to Israel as they were about to go into the Promised Land, Jesus sets before His disciples the ancient choice: the two ways (compare Deut. 30:19; Ps. 1:6; Prov. 14:12; Jer. 21:8). Here are the narrow and wide gates; the easy and the hard ways. Yet this same Jesus later beckoned His disciples, weary of the hard and narrow way, to come to Him, whose yoke is easy and whose burden is light (Mt. 11:28-30). The hard way is easy because it leads to life: the easy way is hard and heavy in the end because it leads to destruction.

7:15-20   In these verses, Christ continued to establish His teaching as the one true way by contrasting it with the claims of other teachers. This was a bold thing to do. Unlike many modern-day teachers, who let students meander through a forest of philosophies without showing them the way out, Christ cut a clear path. He warned His listeners of false prophets. The stupidity and helplessness of sheep was well known in Jesus' day. Sheep were a part of life. So were wolves. The idea of a wolf masquerading as a sheep was the height of cunning and deceit.

A teacher or prophet who disseminates false doctrine does harm, just as a wolf among sheep. Such a person leads people away from God and from the truth that is in Christ. False prophets devour their listeners by plundering innocent minds out of a desire for selfish gain. In Jesus' day, there were many pseudoprophets, just as there are today. People often paid them money or sacrificed other necessities, all for nothing.

For the farmers in Jesus' audience, He threw in another illustration, equally farfetched, but appropriate. The proof of faith is in the fruit of one's life, He told them. Only a good and righteous person bears good fruit (that is, good works). People can spot counterfeit teachers and disciples by the inferior quality of the fruit they produce.

Notice that Christ didn't say the unrighteous won't produce any fruit. Rather, He stressed the difference in the quality of the harvest. "But not everyone who speaks in a spirit is a prophet, except he have the behavior of the Lord. From his behavior, then, the false prophet and the true prophet shall be known" (*Didache* 11:8).

7:21-23 False teachers may teach Jesus' deity, yet remain false teachers in other areas! It takes more than the right words ("Lord, Lord") to make a true prophet. What distinguishes the true prophet and the one who enters the Kingdom is doing the will of the Father. "Lord" (*kurie*) is the title addressed to Jesus in His supreme power at the Last Day.

Who are these whom Jesus will turn away, who have done such great things in Jesus' name? (Notice He does not deny their many and great works, nor does He deny that they were done in His name.) Are not these works (prophesying, casting out demons, doing miracles) the very things Jesus sent His disciples out to do? (See Matthew 10:1; Mark 3:14, 15.)

The reason He turns them away is given in verse 23—He never knew them. And why they were not "known" to Him is also given: they were "evildoers": literally "workers of lawlessness." They did great works but failed to observe the commands of the moral Law, failed thus to do the will of the Father. Perhaps, like the Pharisees (Mt. 23:23, 24), these "evildoers" had neglected the "weightier matters of the law—justice, mercy and faithfulness," while busy with lesser matters "in Jesus' name."

We Christians today can make a comparable mistake, being occupied with many things in Jesus' name—church programs, building plans, or whatever—and neglecting the will of the Father.

7:24-27 Note that the key lies in the two foundations. Luke 6:48 speaks of the man who dug and went deep, and laid a foundation upon the rock. Christ probably told the parable many times, sometimes speaking of digging down to bedrock, and sometimes searching out a rock outcropping.

Note that each man is building something. It is a place he can live in, a "home for his soul" (G. Campbell Morgan). The houses themselves appear well built; the difference is not in their construction. But in one case, the man is, in time, rendered homeless.

The contrast is not between those who hear, and those who don't, but between those who obey when they hear, and those who don't. Bear in mind that the "sayings" of Jesus to be obeyed are those spelled out in the chapters preceding (5-7).

7:28, 29 The "doctrine" of Jesus was the truth He had received from His Father to transmit to the world. "These words you hear are not my own; they belong to the Father who sent me" (Jn. 14:24). Thus He spoke with wisdom that was everlasting.

On the other hand, the Pharisees and scribes taught wisdom that was largely human. They had accumulated hundreds of sayings from the rabbis of the previous few centuries. These sayings had obscured the Law of God, which had been revealed through Moses. Thus the religious leaders were teaching people an inferior wisdom.

The Pharisees taught mostly by lecture, often using intricate arguments. They exalted themselves as experts over the ignorance of those who heard them. Their teaching was mostly done in the synagogue or Temple: essentially, they made people come to them for instruction.

Jesus, on the other hand, went out seeking the lost. He taught people on mountains, in their homes, along the roads, or by the lakeshore. As one who personified the truth He spoke about, His integrity made a deep and lasting impression.

For Discussion

1. Considering the whole context of Matthew 7:13-29, what would you say it means for a prophet to "bear good fruit"? How is this different from preaching what is true, casting out demons, and doing miracles?

2. How might the (rather shocking) distinction between doing great things in Jesus' name and doing the will of the Father (that is, doing Jesus' words) help us establish our priorities?

3. In what ways are you in danger of neglecting the weighty matters of the Law—justice, mercy, and faith?

Window on the Word

Moment of Truth

A certain pastor was ridiculed from time to time—even by other members of the clergy—for his strong belief in Scripture and in Christ. His sermons were always Biblically sound, and he called people repeatedly to turn over their lives to the Lord. He became something of a legend in the community, because he really lived his faith.

One night he received a visit from a fellow pastor—one of his harshest critics—whose teenage daughter was in serious trouble with drugs. It seemed the man's life was falling apart, even though he professed to be a Christian leader.

"Why are you calling on me?" the pastor asked, knowing how this same man had often derided him.

The man looked at him soberly—utterly shaken. "Because you believe in something, and I don't," he answered.

Leader Helps and Lesson Plan

General Guidelines for Group Study

*Open and close each session with prayer.

*Since the lesson texts are not printed in the book, group members should have their Bibles with them for each study session.

*As the leader, prepare yourself for each session through personal study (during the week) of the Bible text and lesson. On notepaper, jot down any points of interest or concern as you study. Jot down your thoughts about how God is speaking to you through the text, and how He might want to speak to the entire group. Look up cross-reference passages (as they are referred to in the lessons), and try to find answers to questions that come to your mind. Also, recall stories from your own life experience that could be shared with the group to illustrate points in the lesson.

*Try to get participation from everyone. Get to know the more quiet members through informal conversation before and after the sessions. Then, during the study, watch for nonverbal signs (a change in expression or posture) that they would like to respond. Call on them. Say: "What are your thoughts on this, Sue?"

*Don't be afraid of silence. Adults need their own space. Often a long period of silence after a question means the group has been challenged to do some real thinking—hard work that can't be rushed!

*Acknowledge each contribution. No question is a dumb question. Every comment, no matter how "wrong," comes from a worthy person, who needs to be affirmed as valuable to the group. Find ways of tactfully accepting the speaker while guiding the discussion back on track: "Thank you for that comment, John, now what do some of the others think?" or, "I see your point, but are you aware of . . . ?"

When redirecting the discussion, however, be sensitive to the fact that sometimes the topic of the moment *should be* the "sidetrack" because it hits a felt need of the participants.

*Encourage *well-rounded* Christian growth. Christians are called to grow in knowledge of the Word, but they are also challenged to grow in love and wisdom. This means that they must constantly develop in their ability to wisely apply the Bible knowledge to their experience.

Lesson Plan

The following four-step lesson plan can be used effectively for each chapter, varying the different suggested approaches from lesson to lesson.

STEP 1: *Focus on Life Need*

The opening section of each lesson is an anecdote, quote, or other device designed to stimulate sharing on how the topic relates to practical daily living. There are many ways to do this. For example, you might list on the chalkboard the group's answers to: "How have you found this theme relevant to your daily life?" "What are your past successes, or failures, in this area?" "What is your present level of struggle or victory with this?" "Share a story from your own experience relating to this topic."

Sharing questions are designed to be open-ended and allow people to talk about themselves. The questions allow for sharing about past experiences, feelings, hopes and dreams, fears and anxieties, faith, daily life, likes and dislikes, sorrows and joys. Self-disclosure results in group members' coming to know each other at a more intimate level. This kind of personal sharing is necessary to experience deep affirmation and love.

However you do it, the point is to get group members to share *where they are now* in relation to the Biblical topic. As you seek to get the group involved, remember the following characteristics of good sharing questions:[1]

1. Good sharing questions encourage risk without forcing participants to go beyond their willingness to respond.

2. Good sharing questions begin with low risk and build toward higher risk. (It is often good, for instance, to ask a history question to start, then build to present situations in people's lives.)

3. Sharing questions should not require people to confess their sins or to share only negative things about themselves.

4. Questions should be able to be answered by every member of the group.

5. The questions should help the group members to know one another better and learn to love and understand each other more.

6. The questions should allow for enough diversity in response so each member does not wind up saying the same thing.

7. They should ask for sharing of self, not for sharing of opinions.

STEP 2: *Focus on Bible Learning*

Use the "Light on the Text" section for this part of the lesson plan. Again, there are a number of ways to get group members involved, but the emphasis here is more on learning Bible content than on applying it. Below are some suggestions on how to proceed. The methods could be varied from week to week.

*Lecture on important points in the Bible passage (from your personal study notes).

*Assign specific verses in the Bible passage to individuals. Allow five or ten minutes for them to jot down 1) questions, 2) comments, 3) points of concern raised by the text. Then have them share in turn what they have written down.

*Pick important or controversial verses from the passage. In advance, do a personal study to find differences of interpretation among commentators. List and explain these "options" on a blackboard and invite comments concerning the relative merits of each view. Summarize and explain your own view, and challenge other group members to further study.

*Have class members do their own outline of the Bible passage. This is done by giving an original title to each section, chapter, and paragraph, placing each under its appropriate heading according to subject matter. Share the outlines and discuss.

*Make up your own sermons from the Bible passage. Each sermon could include: Title, Theme Sentence, Outline, Illustration, Application, Benediction. Share and discuss.

*View works of art based on the text. Discuss.

*Individually, or as a group, paraphrase the Bible passage in your own words. Share and discuss.

*Have a period of silent meditation upon the Bible passage. Later, share insights.

STEP 3: *Focus on Bible Application*

Most adults prefer group discussion above any other learning method. Use the "For Discussion" section for each lesson to guide a good discussion on the lesson topic and how it relates to felt needs.

Students can benefit from discussion in a number of important ways:[2]

1. Discussion stimulates interest and thinking, and helps students develop the skills of observation, analysis, and hope.

2. Discussion helps students clarify and review what they have learned.

3. Discussion allows students to hear opinions that are more mature and perhaps more Christlike than their own.

4. Discussion stimulates creativity and aids students in applying what they have learned.

5. When students verbalize what they believe and are forced to explain or defend what they say, their convictions are strengthened and their ability to share what they believe with others is increased.

There are many different ways to structure a discussion. All have group interaction as their goal. All provide an opportunity to share in the learning process.

But using different structures can add surprise to a discussion. It can mix people in unique ways. It can allow new people to talk.

Total Class Discussion

In some small classes, all students are able to participate in one effective discussion. This can build a sense of class unity, and it allows everyone to hear the wisdom of peers. But in most groups, total class discussion by itself is unsatisfactory because there is usually time for only a few to contribute.

Buzz Groups

Small groups of three to ten people are assigned any topic for discussion. They quickly select a chairperson and a secretary. The chairperson is responsible for keeping the discussion on track, and the secretary records the group's ideas, reporting the relevant ones to the total class.

Brainstorming

Students, usually in small groups, are presented with a problem and asked to come up with as many different solutions as possible. Participants should withhold judgment until all suggestions (no matter how creative!) have been offered. After a short break, the group should pick the best contribution from those suggested and refine it. Each brainstorming group will present its solution in a total class discussion.

Forum Discussion

Forum discussion is especially valuable when the subject is difficult and the students would not be able to participate in a meaningful discussion without quite a bit of background. People with special training or experience have insights which would not ordinarily be available to the students. Each forum member should prepare a three- to five-minute speech and be given uninterrupted time in which to present it. Then students should be encouraged to interact with the speakers, either directly or through a forum moderator.

Debate

As students prepare before class for their parts in a debate, they should remember that it is the affirmative side's repsonsibility to prove that the resolve is correct. The negative has to prove that it isn't. Of course, the negative may also want to present an alternative proposal.

There are many ways to structure a debate, but the following pattern is quite effective.

1. First affirmative speech
2. First negative speech
3. Second affirmative speech
4. Second negative speech
(brief break while each side plans its rebuttal)
5. First negative rebuttal
6. First affirmative rebuttal
7. Second negative rebuttal
8. Second affirmative rebuttal.

Floating Panel

Sometimes you have a topic to which almost everyone in the room would have something to contribute, for example: marriage, love, work, getting along with people. For a change of pace, have a floating panel: four or five people, whose names are chosen at random, will become "experts" for several minutes. These people sit in chairs in the front of the room while you and other class members ask them questions. The questions should be experience related. When the panel has been in front for several minutes, enough time for each person to make several comments, draw other names and replace the original members.

Interview As Homework

Ask students to interview someone during the week and present what they learned in the form of short reports the following Sunday.

Interview in Class

Occasionally it is profitable to schedule an in-class interview, perhaps with a visiting missionary or with someone who has unique insights to share with the group. One person can take charge of the entire interview, structuring and asking questions. But whenever possible the entire class should take part. Each student should write a question to ask the guest.

In-Group Interview

Divide the class into groups of three, called triads. Supply all groups with the same question or discussion topic. A in the group interviews B while C listens. Then B interviews C while A listens. Finally C interviews A while B listens. Each interview should take from one to three minutes. When the triads return to the class, each person reports on what was heard rather than said.

Following every class period in which you use discussion, ask yourself these questions to help determine the success of your discussion time:

1. In what ways did this discussion contribute to the group's understanding of today's lesson?

2. If each person was not involved, what can I do next week to correct the situation?

3. In what ways did content play a role in the discussion? (I.e., people were not simply sharing off-the-top-of-their-head opinions.)

4. What follow-up, if any, should be made on the discussion? (For example, if participants showed a lack of knowledge, or misunderstanding in some area of Scripture, you may want to cover this subject soon during the class hour. Or, if they discussed decisions they were making or projects they felt the class should be involved in, follow-up outside the class hour may be necessary.)

STEP 4: *Focus on Life Response*

This step tries to incorporate a bridge from the Bible lesson to actual daily living. It should be a *specific* suggestion as to "how we are going to *do* something about this," either individually, or as a group. Though this is a goal to aim for, it is unlikely that everyone will respond to every lesson. But it is good to have a suggested life response ready for that one or two in the group who may have been moved by *this* lesson to respond *this week* in a tangible way.

Sometimes a whole group will be moved by one particular lesson to do a major project in light of their deepened understanding of, and commitment to, God's will. Such a response would be well worth the weeks of study that may have preceded it.

Examples of life response activities:

1. A whole class, after studying Scriptural principles of evangelism, decides to host an outreach Bible study in a new neighborhood.

2. As a result of studying one of Paul's prayers for the Ephesians, a group member volunteers to start and oversee a church prayer chain for responding to those in need.

3. A group member invites others to join her in memorizing the key verse for the week.

4. Two group members, after studying portions of the Sermon on the Mount, write and perform a song about peacemaking.

Obviously, only you and your group can decide how to respond appropriately to the challenge of living for Christ daily. But the possibilities are endless.

[1]From *USING THE BIBLE IN GROUPS*, by Roberta Hestenes. © Roberta Hestenes 1983. Adapted and used by permission of Westminster Press, Philadelphia, PA.

[2]The material on discussion methods is adapted from *Creative Teaching Methods*, by Marlene D. LeFever, available from your local Christian bookstore or from David C. Cook Publishing Co., 850 N. Grove Ave., Elgin, IL 60120. Order number: 25254. $14.95. This book contains step-by-step directions for dozens of methods appropriate for use in adult classes.